Preface

The inspiration for this book comes after more than 10 years of helping friends, family, and eventually thousands of consumers, with the tribulations of trying to resolve personal credit problems. The essence of this book is derived from the fact that I am not an attorney nor am I an advocate for the practices of the credit bureaus. Instead, I am a consumer who has experienced and overcome the frustrating, solemn depths of bad credit. I have shared my experiences and techniques with thousands of others, who in return shared what worked best. I then refined and documented which techniques were most *effective*. While struggling to free myself from what seemed to be an eternity of stress and insurmountable problems, I discovered that one could easily use the very same laws that were hindering you, to actually help you. You may ask, is this really legal? Sure, if you don't get caught. I am only joking, it is very legal and very possible. Experian states, "you should dispute all information you feel is not adequately representative of what you believe to be true." Bad information on your credit report not only affects you, but businesses that want to offer you credit, everybody loses. Therefore, challenge everything that is questionable and let the credit bureaus *prove* its accuracy. How many times have you been pulled over for speeding and told by the cop, "by the way, if I don't show up for court, this ticket and fine will be dismissed." The consumers can use this same principle to resolve their own credit problems. The following pages contain only the most efficient, **proven effective**, Step-By-Step instructions on how to resolve derogatory information on your credit reports. Learn to deal with creditors, collectors, debt reduction, rebuilding credit, and Bankruptcy. If you want to read endless pages of legal jargon about the credit laws, this book is NOT for you.

NO PREACHING, JUST TEACHING!!!

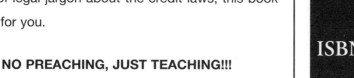

An Educational
Do-It-Yourself

CREDIT REPAIR
KIT

FOURTH
EDITION

ISBN 0-9654345-0-8

Disclaimer & Limited Warranty

Please note that I am not an attorney and the following information is based on a great deal of experience, research, and existing laws. Therefore the information contained in this kit is believed to be reliable but not guaranteed due to differing interpretations and changes in laws and regulations. Purchases made <u>directly</u> through Sainz Enterprises, LLC may be returned *within* 30 days with a sales receipt to place of purchase for a full refund of the purchase price, or current sale price, which ever is lowest at the time of your return. This warranty is valid <u>**only**</u> for purchases through Sainz Enterprises, LLC. Second and third party resellers <u>*may not*</u> offer a return guarantee or have differing return policies than Sainz Enterprises, LLC due to the addition of other promotional materials sold along with this kit. It is the responsibility of the purchaser to inquire at time of purchase regarding returns and refunds. Users should use this material at their own discretion. I always recommend that you seek the services of a competent attorney, should you feel your circumstances warrant the need for legal advice. It should also be understood that the author, distributor, and retailer are not responsible nor liable to any individual or parties for any damages or losses caused by or allegedly caused by the use of this book/kit to the extent of the purchase price of the kit. This kit may not be reproduced in part or whole without written permission from Joe P. Sainz III, except for the provided forms that may be reproduced for the use of the purchaser only. Use of the kit constitutes agreement of afore mentioned terms.

Utilizing the best resource for restoring your credit...you!

inspiration

DEDICATION

I am continually amazed by the speed of each passing day. Bewildered at times but never lost, I wake up happy and anxious to conquer another day. I could not feel this way if it weren't for the unbelievable amount of confidence instilled in me by my beautiful wife, three stunning daughters, and vivacious son. It is because of them that I can dream the impossible dream. If one day I woke up homeless and penniless the one thing that I know I could never lose would be their Love and Support. This and everything I do is for you!

Introduction

New age of credit restoration...1

The Credit System

Credit Reporting Process...5

Consumer Credit Reporting Act...5

Fair Credit Reporting Act...5

Federal Trade Commission...6

Seven Year Cycle Defined...6

Importance of Date of Last Activity...6

Federal Equal Credit Opportunity Act...7

Consumer Credit Protection Act...7

Point System Example...8

Credit Reports- Obtaining & Translating

The (3) Main Credit Bureaus...11

Importance of Three Credit Reports...11

Importance of 60 Day Response Period...12

Free Credit Reports For Credit Denial...12

Caution Calling The Credit Bureau...13

Obtaining Credit Reports Free & Fee...13

Translating Credit Reports...13

The (4) Main Areas of a Credit Report...14

Disputing-How to do it Effectively

What is Disputing?...19

Your Rights as a Consumer...20

The Rights of the Credit Bueaus...21

Credit Report Information Defined...21

Step-By-Step Disputing Instructions...21

The Fair Credit Billing Act...22

What Exactly To Dispute...23

Specific Credit Report Items

Adding 100 Word Comment To Report...27

Personal Section Defined...28

Inquires Defined...30

Basic Credit Accounts Defined...33

Category (1) Type of Accounts...33

Category (2) Type of Accounts...34

Medical Accounts & Student Loans...35-36

Public Record Items Defined...38

Child Support, Divorce, & Felonies...39

Repossessions and Foreclosures...41

The IRS & Civil Judgements...42

Tax Liens & Wage Garnishments...43

Understanding Bankruptcy

What types of Bankruptcy are there...47

What are the Effects of a Bankruptcy...47

Choosing the Bankruptcy Right For You...48

Chapter 7 Bankruptcy Details...49

Chapter 13 Bankruptcy Details...49

Do-It-Yourself or Get Help...50

Compromising with Creditors

What is the Purpose of a Compromise...55

How You Make a Compromise...55

What To Ask For in a Compromise ...55

Handling Collection Agencies

How To STOP Them Cold...59

The Fair Debt Collection Practices Act...59

The Cease Communication Letter...59

The Rights of You and The Collector...59

Credit Collector Limitations...60

Resolving 'Bad' Checks

Bounced Check - Creditor to Collections...63

Step-By-Step Instructions for Resolution...63

Preventing Credit Report Damage...64

Debt Reduction & Lowering Your Bankcard APR

Debt Reduction Overview...69

Eight Best Debt Reduction Plans...69

Choosing Which Plan Is Best For You...69

Balance Piracy Defined...70

Who is Eligible to Lower Their A.P.R....71

Lowering A.P.R. Instructions...72

The Big Savings...74

Rebuilding your credit with Secured & Unsecured Credit Cards

How to Start Rebuilding Your Credit...77

What is a Secured Credit Card...77

Benefits of a Secured Credit Card...77

Obtaining Gas Cards...77

Using our list of Secured Credit Cards...77

What To Do and What Not To Do...78

Special Interest

Sainz Publishing Legal Kits...81

PCMailer Promotions...83

Free Internet Offers...85

Offers to Rebuild your Credit...87

Look Here...89

Frequently Asked Questions

What is this section about...93

Actual questions asked by consumers...93

Cut To The Chase

Who should use this section...115

What will you be able to accomplish...115

What am I missing in this section...115

Step-by-Step Instructions...115

Appendix

Equifax Phone Number & Address...App-1

Trans Union Phone Number & Address...App-1

Experian Phone Number & Address...App-1

Federal Trade Commission Phone No...App-2

Office of the Controller of the Currency...App-2

Federal Reserve Board...App-2

Internal Revenue Service...App-2

Sample Figures 1 thru 7...App-3-15

Complete Bankcard List...App-17

Glossary of Terms...App-19

Introduction

In August of 1997, Governor Roy Romer of Colorado set precedence for the nation in what is now slated the The Credit-Reporting Bill. The millennium has shown us even more progress in credit reporting reform. After many years of frustration and complaints, the prayers of millions of consumers were answered by Governor Romer's reforms to a failing credit reporting system. "Consumer-credit reporting agencies that do sloppy work could face costly fines under a bill strongly opposed by the industry..."

The problems with the current credit reporting system finally hit home. Some of the biggest supporters of this bill were congressional leaders from Colorado. It should be considered a embarrassment that it actually took our elected representatives until 1997 to figure out that the complaints of the consumers regarding the practices of the credit bureaus were actually well warranted. The wheels of change weren't put into motion until a couple of family members of senators and representatives were actually affected by the lacking current credit system. The changes required to update the current system will definitely take some time. But Experian, formerly known as TRW, has made the greatest strives to reduce the possibilities for errors in the system. Believe it or not, Experian now encourages consumers to dispute all information that is believed to misleading or inaccurate in any way. The old side door and shell game of doing things is quickly becoming ways of the past.

"It is time to take control, and repair your credit yourself."

The internet is revolutionizing how everyday tasks are accomplished. People have an immeasurable wealth of information and knowledge just a few key strokes away from them at any time. Information on credit restoration can be found almost anywhere on the internet. This ability to ascertain information brings new challenges to the credit reporting system. We as consumers are expanding our abilities to gain information and make better, more informed decisions. This book is a testament to technology summarizing experience with an ever expanding knowledge base obtained from the internet and credit professionals who now find their home on-line. The internet and the millennium have brought us the ability to comparatively evaluate the most effective means to resolve credit problems in a matter of seconds. Bottom line, you have before you one of the best tools that can be offered to the consumer to assist with the hassles of resolving your credit dilemmas. It is time to take control and Repair Your Credit Yourself.

This kit will not only teach you how to successfully dispute (remove) items from your credit report, but will also teach you:

- how to stop debt collectors,
- provide you with tactics on how to make compromises with creditors
- how to resolve bad checks
- lower your bankcard a.p.r. in five minutes
- provide you with debt reduction plans
- special section on bankruptcy
- rebuilding your credit with secured credit cards
- list of banks offering secured and unsecured bankcards
- special interest and opportunities
- frequently asked questions
- 'cut to the chase' section for those on the go
- the forms to do it all

I make no false promises or claims. For most, this process will not provide results overnight but never the less is very effective. Even if you have had a bankruptcy recently this book can help you! If you are diligent in your efforts and follow the procedures as outlined in this kit, you will separate yourself from the tens of millions of people who are still suffering from bad credit. My biggest emphasis to you is to be PATIENT. Your present credit situation took time to evolve. Now getting yourself out of this credit dilemma is going to take time as well. You have now taken the right step by getting help and can now begin the process of improving your quality of life. What lies ahead is your devotion of time and effort, and as they say, "if you want something done right, you have to **Do It Yourself**."

This kit begins with a brief description of how the credit system functions, where you fit in, and what you need to know and do to resolve your particular situation. The kit also describes the laws that were enacted by congress and how they affect you. These laws were designed with you in mind; so don't be afraid to use the powers of the system to get yourself out of the situation you put yourself in. There is no problem to big or to small that is not covered in the book. We have helped consumers with every imaginable credit problem, just look within.

I **highly recommended** this kit to people who believe they have good credit. Most people are very surprised by what they learn from this book, especially those thinking they have perfect credit. If you ask Senator Joan Johnson, you will find that she wasn't very pleased when she was embarrassingly rejected for credit at Nordstroms. I can't emphasis enough that you must review your credit reports at least once, if not twice a year, for inaccuracies, good credit or bad. If there is a problem, you will at least become aware of it immediately instead of finding out by surprise.

The practices and recommendations within this kit are all **LEGAL** and are proven successful through experience! But, **it is up to you** to put them to use. With this in mind, lets get started on **Repairing Your Credit**!

The Credit System

Before solving any problem, one must first understand the problem, and then determine the best means for solving the problem. When dealing with the credit system, the first step is to understand exactly how credit reporting works.

There are three major credit bureaus Experian, Equifax, and Trans Union. All three are private businesses that have no government affiliation. Like any other business, they are in existence because there is a very profitable market for what they do. They receive information, maintain it and sell it. All three of these bureaus consider you nothing more than a name and a number. But you must never forget that there is strength in numbers, and this is exactly what we will use to our advantage, as I will explain later.

Between the three bureaus and their subsidiaries, they handle the credit histories of everyone in the United States. Being that they handle such an enormous amount of information between them, do you suppose that any one of them could have made an error in your file? Congress without a doubt recognized the enormous power and influence that such businesses could exercise over society and each consumer. For these reasons, congress enacted a series of Federal laws that protect the rights of the consumer as well as govern the actions of all credit bureaus, creditors and collection agencies.

The Consumer Credit Protection Act (CCPA) is one law in a series that is designed as a tool for the consumer. This tool ensures that the personal information maintained by the credit bureaus is absolutely 100% accurate. If credit bureaus do not comply with the act, the consumer can intercede into the functions of the credit bureaus. The consumer can then make necessary corrections to their credit reports to reflect their preexisting level of credit accuracy.

The Most important law enacted by the Federal Trade Commission is **The Fair Credit Reporting Act (FCRA)**. This law specifically applies to the credit bureaus and creditors. The way this law works is that whenever you apply and receive credit, even if it is for the first time, the information is recorded by the credit bureau(s). If it is your first time, the credit bureau will then establish a credit report for you, thus starting your **credit history** and a documented account of all your personal and non-personal credit transactions. Creditors can then obtain the information from the bureau and send information back updating the bureau periodically about the most recent activities on your account. The Fair Credit Reporting Act specifies exactly how this information is obtained, recorded, stored and sold to other possible creditors. The FCRA holds the credit bureaus responsible for this task and is specific on how these functions must be carried out. Any deviations from the prescribed law could ultimately result in legal action taken against the credit bureau. For this reason, you deal directly with the credit bureau and **not** the creditor, when trying to resolve a problem on your credit report. The

The Fair Credit Reporting Act is a federal law that will allow the consumer to intervene into any business practice that openly offers credit information on individual consumers.

Average family credit card debt carries a balance of $4,800.00 with 4 credit cards.

"When the Fair Credit Reporting Act was enacted, it was determined that items recorded on your credit report shall remain there for seven years, except for bankruptcies and certain other court affiliated matters which will remain for ten"

reason for this is simple; the creditors don't handle your credit report, the credit bureaus do (Experian, Equifax, and Trans Union)!

When the <u>Fair Credit Reporting Act</u> was enacted, it was determined that items recorded on your credit report shall remain there for **seven years, except for certain BANKRUPTCIES,** which remain for **ten** years (this topic will be covered in more detail later). For example, if you had an account with a creditor and it went bad (perhaps you were unable to pay, laid off, hospitalized, overextended, or simply refused to pay your bill), it can be reported to the credit bureau as a derogatory (**BAD**) account for seven years. The biggest question for consumers is when does the **seven year** period begin and end? The Federal Trade Commission took on the task of answering that very question.

One of the many jobs of **The Federal Trade Commission (FTC)** as a regulatory government agency is to oversee the proper practices of the credit bureaus. The FTC has written a document called *"The FTC's Interpretation Of The Fair Credit Reporting Act".* This legal document describes in detail the defining lines of the **Seven Year Cycle.** The term: *The date of last activity* appears in the document and refers to the exact day when the seven year period begins. *The date of last activity* is defined as <u>the date of your last charge on the account</u> **or** <u>the date of your last payment</u>. With this in mind, it is very important to consider the dates that are associated with every line of credit on your credit report, whether the report is good or bad. If you feel the dates don't coincide with the seven year cycle for any particular item, you must take quick advantage of the law to stop further damage to your credit history. It is up to the credit bureaus to correct or **remove** any information on your report that is even slightly wrong. This includes dates and any other pertinent data associated with <u>each</u> line on your credit report. Checking the dates for accuracy on each item of your credit report is a great starting point for uncovering inaccuracies. For some reason correctly recording dates on your credit report has proven to be a problem. Who's at fault for this error is overshadowed by the fact that you now have a great reason to have this item disputed and removed due to inaccuracies.

Hopefully, you have kept good records on all of your accounts and you can produce evidence such as a money order receipt, returned check, or billing statement to reaffirm The date of last activity on your account. We would like to believe that all creditors are honest when it comes to adhering to the seven year cycle and your rights. But truthfully, it can be beneficial to the creditors to maintain 'charged off accounts' (accounts that the creditor has been unable to collect payment on, thus closed) in their system of records (even though its illegal). So always question dates for there validity. Not all creditors are perpetrators of this act but there are a few major credit card issuers that feel the need to make this a standard practice. So don't be surprised if you discover one.

If you realize the credit bureau or the creditor has made an error and it is not rectified to your satisfaction after adequate attempts of resolution (disputing), I recommend that you contact your local Federal Trade Commission. The FTC is an enormous legal entity and completely at your disposal. You can place a legal complaint with the FTC for **FREE** with the assurance that it will be handled appropriately. The credit bureaus follow the strict guide lines pretty closely, but there is always human error. The FTC is always very supportive in resolving your claim. In figure 1 of the appendix, you will find a phone number to the central office of the Federal Trade Commission. You may contact anyone at the provided number and ask them for further instructions on placing a claim with their office.

Another important aspect of credit bureaus and other prospective credit issuing establishments (major credit cards, banks, retailers, etc.) is how they go about evaluating the quality of your credit history. All of the credit bureaus and credit issuing establishments evaluate you on a point system. The **Federal Equal Credit Opportunity Act** prohibits creditors from discriminating against all applicants on the basis of race, color, religion, national origin, sex, marital status, age (provided that the applicant has the capacity to enter into a binding contract); because all or part of the applicant's income derives from any public assistance program; or because the applicant has in good faith exercised any right under the **Consumer Credit Protection Act**.

Although each credit company has their own technique or system of scoring you, you better believe that there is some type of point system being used to see if you meet their standards of credit stability. I can't offer you each and every technique used out there, but what I can offer you is an example to give you some idea of how they may set up a scoring system. This is my own example and you should not assume that everyone is using this particular point system. The idea behind this scoring system is to measure credit stability, the higher you score the more likely you are to be recognized as a potential receiver of credit.

The Federal Trade Commission will quickly respond to any complaints that you may have concerning the practices of any creditor, collection agency, or credit bureau.

Assessing Credit Stability

Point System Example

ITEM	POINTS
AGE	
18-24	1
25-65	2
OVER 65	1

ITEM	POINTS
DEPENDENTS	
No dependents	0
1-3 dependents	3
4+ dependents	2

ITEM	POINTS
TYPE OF WORK	
Professional/Executive	4
Skilled worker	3
Blue collar	2
Other	1

ITEM	POINTS
STABILITY	
0-1 years @ same address	0
1-4 years @ same address	1
4+ years @ same address	2

ITEM	POINTS
CREDIT EXPERIENCE	
Good credit w/this lender	5
Good credit w/another lender	3
Checking account.	1
Savings account	2

ITEM	POINTS
MONTHLY OBLIGATIONS	
Less than $500	2
More than $500	1

HOW DID YOU DO?

18 points or more	Usually approved
15-17 points	Further review required
Below 15 points	Declined

ITEM	POINTS
PREVIOUS ADDRESS	
4 years or less	1
More than 4 years	2
Telephone in your name	2

ITEM	POINTS
EMPLOYMENT	
1 year or less @ present job	1
1-3 years @ present job	2
4-7 years @ present job	1
7 or more years @ present job	2
Filing jointly w/working spouse	2

Credit Reports: Obtaining & Translating

Now that you are familiar with the laws that govern the credit reporting system you should be familiar with the form in which your credit history is recorded. I am assuming that almost everyone has either gone into a store or have been sent an application for a line credit. Once you fill out a credit application and return it to the creditor, you have just entered or reentered the credit system. Something as simple as getting a phone in your name will get you into the system. The credit system is very basic. Every time you open an account with your name and social security no. a record of your action is recorded. These actions are reported by the creditor to the credit bureaus who then record them in a computer file (CREDIT REPORT), which will remain open until you die. Your file is constantly updated every time you submit information to a participating creditor, meaning every time you pay a bill your file is updated. After a short period of time in the credit system a creditor can evaluate your file, using a technique as the point system, and determine how responsible you are. As you seen before, how well you score is determined by the amount of positive items, negative items, and extent and time periods of each item in your file. If you always pay your bills late and have had three jobs in the past year you will be considered irresponsible and a bad credit risk, this is BAD CREDIT. If you have recently been denied credit you may safely assume that you have a credit dilemma, if you are not already aware of it. The **FIRST STEP** in resolving your credit dilemma is finding out exactly where the problem is. You do this by obtaining your credit reports (credit file/history) from **ALL 3** credit reporting agencies. It is very important to note that if you are married, you must obtain credit reports for you and your spouse. The reason for this is simple; you have two different social security numbers. Even though you may have joint credit accounts or file taxes together, you are still two separate identities in the eyes of the credit bureaus. You may share similar credit information but this does not mean that corrections made on one credit report will automatically be reflected on your spouses credit report. Therefore, order credit reports for **BOTH** of you!

Never forget that there are three main credit bureaus that are not at all affiliated with each other. In fact, all three of them are competitors in the same business and they DO NOT share information. Because of this, it is very common for each of the credit bureaus to have varying information on you. Some bureaus may not have information on you at all. One of many reasons for this may be that they are not as prominent in one area of the US as another. But, the more likely reason is just by coincidence. Like I stated before, the bureaus are independent businesses that have differing clientel. Thus, the particular businesses that you have made purchases from or have got credit through, have contracts with the varying bureaus, maybe just one of them or in some cases all of them. They have to pay to have access to their databanks, therefore they may just use one of the credit bureaus. This is why items may appear on just one of the credit reports.

Important Note: In order to accurately restore your credit, you must obtain your credit reports from all three credit bureaus, and if your married, for your spouse as well.

Your Credit Report

"When you receive your credit reports, whatever you do, DO NOT *procrastinate in going over them, you only have 60 days before they are considered outdated."*

Another important fact to note is that each of the creditors report to the credit bureaus periodically. The report period for each creditor may vary. Some creditors report to the bureaus semi-annually, quarterly, or even monthly. Therefore, even if you have obtained a credit report recently, it is a very good idea to obtain the latest report from all three of the agencies at the same time to insure you get the most recent changes on your credit report. By having all three of your reports in front of you at the same time, you are able to compare the differences between the three of them. If one of the agencies returns a letter to you stating for example, "they don't have any record of you", don't get excited, this is just one less thing that you have to worry about correcting.

When you receive your credit reports, whatever you do, **DON'T** procrastinate in going over them. According to a FCRA, you only have **60 DAYS TO RESPOND** to items on your credit report before they consider the information to be outdated and no longer valid. This **60-DAY** stipulation goes back to the periodic reporting process of the creditor. The bureaus assume that new information is likely to have been added to your credit report in the past **60 DAYS** thus outdating the old information.

If a creditor has recently turned you down, you probably received a letter stating the reasons why and from whom they obtained your credit history. Because of your decline of credit, you are entitled to receive a **FREE** credit report if you request it within **60 DAYS** from the time of decline. This report is free from the credit-reporting bureau which provided the creditor with the information. You are only entitled **one** free credit report per decline, and **ONLY FROM THAT INDIVIDUAL BUREAU.** For instance, you applied to ABC credit card and they sent you a letter of decline. Somewhere on that letter, usually in the middle, you will see a name like Experian, Equifax, or some other credit-reporting bureau I have not previously mentioned. These are the people you need to contact in order to receive your free credit report (**see figures 1-4 in the appendix for the desired sample letter**). In the case that the credit bureau listed on your decline letter is different from the three main bureaus (Experian etc..), don't worry, you handle them all the same way. I had mentioned earlier that the three main bureaus have subsidiaries or smaller offices in almost every major city. These smaller offices share or access the exact same information from the main computer files belonging to one of the three main credit reporting bureaus. There are many of these smaller credit-reporting companies throughout the U.S. that have contracts with the (3) main credit bureaus. These companies only buy and sell your credit information. So if the name of the credit bureau on your decline letter is foreign to you, call the credit bureau on the decline letter to verify which larger bureau they are affiliated with. By doing this you can be reassured that you have all of your necessary credit reports, when it comes time to make corrections. One thing to always remember when contacting **ANY** credit bureau by phone, you must be very careful of what you say.

SECTION TWO

Sometimes you can damage yourself when you contact a credit bureau by phone. The representatives assisting you are trained to ask specific questions in order to extract information. The information that they may get out of you, or that you may accidentally tell them, may come back and harm you in the future. Just remember, **DON'T** get into any conversations with these people. Simply get the information that you need and end your call. For instance, if you haven't received your report within <u>two-three weeks</u> from ordering, which is more than sufficient time, you should call and inquire about the reasons for the delay. Remember, be very careful! If calls are made, you should always keep a record of them and their content. Try and always correspond with credit bureaus by mail, or with the advent of the internet, by e-mail.

As soon as you do receive your credit reports make **several copies** of each so that you can use one of them as a work sheet and save one for your records. Another thing, you must realize how many people that each bureau is handling and be a little bit patient. When your reports do reach you, **DON'T** become enraged at the sight of their content and pick up the phone to complain to the bureaus. After all, they only control how the information is handled -- and **NOT** necessarily what has been reported. Allow this kit and your persistence to handle the task of getting rid of the bad information that your creditors have placed on your report.

If you <u>WERE NOT</u> recently denied credit, insurance, or employment due to your credit history, you must obtain your credit reports in the standard fashion, pay for them. In April of 1992 Experian began offering one free credit report to each consumer per year. As of September of 1996, 5 million credit reports were issued for free. The free report plan was discontinued with the passing of the FCRA update of September 1996. The new law states that free credit reports will be provided once a year to those individual consumers that can verify that they are unemployed and seeking employment, receiving public welfare assistance, or believe that their credit file contains inaccuracies resulting from fraud. Otherwise all three of the credit bureaus require that you pay a fee of $8.00 for each report. **Figures 2-4 of the appendix will detail the format for ordering your all of your credit reports and where to send them.** Be sure and supply each of the credit bureaus with all the required information as indicated on the example figures. Definitely, don't forget to sign each of them. Your request must be accompanied with a check or money order in the amount of $8.00, never send cash. The phone numbers and addresses of each of the credit bureaus are located in **figure 1 of the appendix**, at the rear of the kit.

Once you receive **ALL** of your credit reports, the initial part of **STEP ONE** is complete. It may be difficult, but you must refrain yourself from becoming angry and frustrated at the condition of your reports. Believe me when

You are only entitled to a free credit report from the issuing credit bureau that was used to obtain information on you that lead to a decline of credit, employment, or insurance.

Stay Calm!

13

"The Experian reports are more easily understood and are good to start with so that you can learn how the reports are read in preparation for other reports."

There have been a lot of improvements made lately to the old types of credit reports to ease the confusion of the consumer.

I tell you that your problems are not as bad as you think. I have seen many reports and those of the extremely wealthy tend to be the worst. It just goes to show that sometimes the bigger your wealth, the bigger your credit problems. So just maintain your cool and follow my instructions very closely, and **YOU WILL** produce the results that you desire.

There is no easy trick to translate the information on your credit reports from garble to logic. Translation of your credit reports may be more difficult for some more than others. But, the most effective way I have found to help people understand the information on their credit reports is to first go over the three reports and take note of how each report is laid out. Each of the credit bureaus formats their credit reports differently from each other. They all provide the same basic sections of information, but format their credit reports differently. Take Trans Union. They locate your entire personal information section at the top of the very first page where it is easily located. But, the way they organize the rest of your credit information is far more difficult to understand than the other two bureaus. Experian is the best when it comes to ease in understanding and locating information on your credit reports. Experian numbers each item then provides all the important information about each item in clear complete sentences, no confusing columns. Equifax is fairly easy to understand, even though they use columns and locate your personal information at the beginning and end of the report. All three bureaus may also vary in the information they disclose. For instance, **one credit bureau may place a judgment for child support**, or perhaps, your **monthly salary** on your credit report. Yes, this is a common legal practice, but is it truly necessary?

Next you should take just one of the credit reports and the explanatory literature provided, and slowly go over the example. I strongly suggest that you use **Experian's** credit report and literature first. Experian has set the standard for credit report formats with their style of describing each item on the credit report. Experian also provides you with an additional information and fact sheet. This sheet explains how they have characterized some parts of your credit account history and answers a few commonly asked questions. By using Experian's report first, you can familiarize yourself with what type of information should be contained within each item of your report. Using Experian first, makes the transition to the formats of the other credit bureaus a little easier. When you get to the other two credit reports, the differences with layout and organization of specific item information, will become more obvious. The Experian reports will teach you what information should be found in each item of your credit report so that you can read the more difficult reports. Once you know what should be in the reports, figuring out the more difficult reports and how they are formatted should be a lot easier. There have been a lot of improvements made lately to the old types of credit reports to ease the confusion of the consumer.

When you get to the reports of Equifax and Trans Union, pick an item from the Experian report that you thoroughly understand and that is also listed on the Equifax and Trans Union report. By knowing what information should be disclosed about this item from Experian's report, you should gradually be able to understand how they have listed the same information on the other reports. The other two credit bureaus use a lot credit bureau language and abbreviations to describe your credit information. For example, they use a (R) to designate a revolving account, like a SEARS revolving account. They use a (I) to show that it's an installment account like a loan. Another use of the acronym (I), not to be confused with its use for an installment account, is to indicate if the account is an individual (I) or a joint (J) account. To assist the consumer with the column format and continual use of abbreviations, these bureaus will furnish you with an example report that explains how their information is recorded. They will also provide you with a definition sheet, which explains all of the abbreviations, and codes they use. You should take the example they provided and study it until you feel comfortable with the format. Carefully notice how and where the different areas of information are laid-out in these credit reports.

It is very easy to locate all of your **Personal** information, but pay close attention to the other areas. You will notice on the example that there are certain items that are distinguished by the attached note, or abbreviation, "**Inquiry.**" The other two sections are: **Basic Credit** (Bank Credit Cards, Merchandise Stores, Banks Loans, etc...) and things of **Public Record** (Tax Liens, Bankruptcies, Judgments, etc...). Equifax and Trans Union will usually distinguish these specific areas of information by associating a note or heading of some kind with each of them. For example, there might be an item listed as Rockview Bank with the note "**Inquiry**" associated with it. This tells you that Rockview Bank took a look at your credit report on the date indicated. An example of a Public Record item may be something like **Denver Cnty Ct.-BK 13** filed. This means that a bankruptcy preceding was filed in Denver county court on the date indicated. Keep in mind; <u>ANYTHING</u> that involves the court system is a matter of public record and subject to placement on your credit report. We will cover all of these areas and more in the following sections.

When you have reached the point where you are comfortable in understanding each item on all of your credit reports, and you can recognize problems that seem to exist with certain items, it's time for us to move on to the next **VERY** important section of this kit.

DISPUTING!!!

Remember, don't get excited and fly off the handle if you see something on your report that doesn't look right. Use the laws designed to protect you. I

As of September of 1997, and 5 million credit reports later, Experian no longer issues free credit reports, unless you have special circumstances or hardships, or live in a few select states that have exemptions to this law.

"...even if you do have good credit, or believe you do, it is recommended that you obtain all three of your credit reports at least once a year..."

am giving you this advise at the end of this section because I want you to remember it clearly. If you have any account that has already been charged off or sent to collections, don't pay it without going over **SECTIONS 5 & 6** of this kit. Payment of these types of accounts will only restart the clock on the **seven year cycle**, dragging your problem out that much longer. If you do encounter any further problems, or have a question about the explanatory literature, or have questions about the report itself, the credit bureaus will be glad to assist you.

Also remember, even if you do have good credit, or believe you do, it is recommended that you obtain all three of your credit reports at least once a year to do routine maintenance like cleaning off inquires and old information. If there exists a problem, you can catch it before you are surprised by a decline letter for credit. There is a lot of fraud going on these days so Beware!

Please refer to the appendix for **The Glossary of Terms** for detailed information on credit terms and definitions.

Disputing: How to do it effectively

This section is probably the most important section of the kit! The reason for its importance is simple. This is the section where you as a consumer are instructed how to exercise your **RIGHTS** under the previously mentioned credit law (CCRA). The legal term for exercising your rights to have corrections made to your credit history is called **DISPUTING**.

I must inform you that disputing items on your credit report is a very delicate procedure that is best handled a few items at a time. It is possible to reach your goal, but if you are over anxious and try and do too much at once, you may fail. The credit bureaus also have rights when it comes to disputing, but usually will not exercise them if your requests appear to be professional and legitimate. Not that your requests are not legitimate, but lets face it, you purchased this kit with the intentions that you may be able to get rid of a few items that have proven to be a stumbling block in your path towards a new car or a home. Allow me to explain. If you use the disputing procedure that I am about to give to you to try and remove 90% of your bad credit information all at once, you may be disappointed to learn that the credit bureau is **NOT** going to take you seriously. The credit bureau will simply send you a letter stating that nothing has been done at this time because they consider your request to be "*Frivolous and Irrelevant,*" basically a joke. This is only logical and within the law. Otherwise, there would be no such thing as bad credit. Everybody would simply go in debt, claim bankruptcy, and then remove it from their credit history as if it never happened. On the other hand, if you're patient and smart, and make only a *few* requests at a time, you may be consistently rewarded with success and ultimately achieve your future goals.

Now, if you have been one of those unfortunate victims of fraud, where your name and social No. were stolen and used to obtain credit, by all means dispute the items and charges and inform the all legal authorities at once. You may have to submit a police report and all formal correspondences in regards to this matter in order to rectify your credit history. If your credit problems have been self-induced, then I recommend you mix up your requests. For example, your first try with the process may be to submit a few common requests like address updates, late payment corrections, removal of ex-spouses names, removal of outdated accounts, and a single major problem like a bankruptcy. This type of request is not lengthy and generally will be handled by the credit bureau as a legitimate request. You may have to dispute the same item more than once before it is removed. Just keep this in mind that your credit problems didn't appear overnight and they will take time to resolve as well. The whole idea behind disputing is to force the credit bureaus to do verifications on every item of question.

It's in your best interest to use the advantages of the system to relieve yourself of the responsibility of contacting a creditor. In other words, dispute any

When disputing, keep in mind that if you try and include 90% of your credit report in your dispute as inaccurate, you stand a very good chance of receiving back a letter that basically says nothing on your credit report has changed because your claims are outrageous and unbelievable.

Give it time to resolve.

"Disputing is the most efficient way, if not the only way, to clear up your credit history."

suspicious item FIRST! You shouldn't have to call or write any creditor at this point. Wait for the results of your initial dispute to come back. In many cases your problem will be resolved by this first action. Use the methods of this kit and the credit laws before resorting to any other actions.

Disputing is the most efficient way, if not the only way, to clear up your credit history. Don't waste your time arguing on the phone with an old creditor when you don't have to. In some instances, you can be doing yourself more damage than good by contacting these creditors. Your account by this point may have been sent to another location, erased, or even lost and unobtainable entirely. By calling them, you are not only giving them reason to inquire, but you are putting yourself in a time disadvantage. You are at a time disadvantage because you have just destroyed the element of surprise. You want to catch everyone you are disputing as unprepared as possible. Remember, if they can't verify a disputed item within 30 days, **LEGITIMATE OR NOT**, it must be removed as **YOU REQUESTED!** A successful dispute always begins knowing *what*, *when*, and *how* to dispute an item.

You now have an idea of *when* to dispute, but knowing *what* to dispute is very important as well. Recall the famous quote, "chance favors the prepared mind." If you know exactly what should be contained in every line of information, chances are you will be better prepared at spotting an error. I am certain you have realized that there is an astounding amount of information contained in each of your credit reports. But, you must also be aware that each item or line contains separate segments of information. For instance, a line of information from a creditor like Visa will have separate information segments like:

- Creditors name
- Type of account
- Date opened
- Terms of account
- Credit limit
- Account balance
- Payment record
- Amount past due
- Account No.
- Creditors identification No.
- Account status
- Single or joint acount
- DATE OF LAST ACTIVITY

The way this information is recorded holds true for all four of the major information groups. i.e. Personal, Basic Credit, Inquires, and Public Records (court affiliated). The Law works this way, **every bit of information contained in every line of every report, must be absolutely 100% correct, otherwise it must be _Removed_**. If you successfully dispute some information and it happens to be a public record item like bankruptcy, it will **stay off forever**. If any personal information is changed or updated by you, **it will remain that way**. The only type of information that _may_ reappear after a successful dispute is basic credit information. This group of information will usually stay off of your credit report 70-80% of the time. The reason an item may reappear after a successful dispute is due to the creditor. Even though the credit bureau is bound by law to remove items that cannot be verified within 30 days, the creditors may at a later date find just cause to place the item back on our report. Don't let this discourage you. If this happens, simply apply the process again after a few months. Eventually, you will achieve your goal, and the item will be removed.

When you have all of your credit reports in front of you, you must begin the tedious process of going over every item on each report, and determine if there are **ANY** possible errors contained in **ANY** segment of every line. If there is the slightest doubt in your mind whether something is correct, or you simply think that a payment was only 29 days late, and not 30 as they recorded, **DISPUTE IT** and make them verify it or remove it. You are not obligated to prove anything, **THEY ARE**! It's the same as being accused of a crime; you are innocent of bankruptcy until <u>proven</u> guilty. In this case, if the <u>credit bureau</u> cannot verify your credit discrepancy within 30 days, they must remove it. And as I stated above, if the item removed is a public record item like a bankruptcy, it's gone forever from your credit history. The best way to begin this process is as follows:

1) Take one of the photocopies of your report (you should have made several by this point), several pens, varying colors of Hi-Liters, and begin clearly numbering each item on your report. Remember handle each credit report separately.

2) Go through with one of your Hi-Liters and mark **ANY** and **ALL** discrepancies associated with each numbered item. You should alternate the color of your hi-lighter with every line, being sure to hi-light the item number with the same pen. If you feel a numbered item of your report is **absolutely 100% correct, DON'T** hi-light it, just skip it.

3) Since this is one of your scratch credit reports, you can go ahead and make your notes next to the items you feel to be incorrect or just use a separate piece of paper. The notes to yourself should identify what you feel to be wrong with the hi-lighted item. I will provide you with some sample dispute phrases so that you can correspond them with each of your items of dispute. The sample dispute phrases will be included with each area of importance contained in section four. If your notes are clear, it will make it that much easier to correspond your item of dispute to a related sample phrase.

4) Prepare your <u>original</u> credit report reflecting the work done on the scratch report. The original copy should be neatly numbered and hi-lighted, remember no notes on this copy.

5) Type up your letter using **figure 5** as an example. Your letter will have a

The credit bureaus are bound by law to remove items that cannot be verified within 30 days. If a certain public record item is removed from your credit report it cannot be placed back on!

Remove it for good!

NOTE

You are allowed to write the reason for the dispute or changes directly on the original report next to the item being disputed, or in an area provided on the report and send it in. This practice is effective, but I recommend that you use the provided forms and procedures of this kit because of proven effectivness.

simple opening statement followed by an itemized list that corresponds in number to the items noted on your original credit report. The list will contain items you request to be changed, updated, or deleted.

6) Send in your letter and your hi-lighted original credit report with the letter appearing first. Certified mail is not necessary. Repeat this procedure for each credit report.

NOTE- (Although we recommend you write your own letter of dispute, when you do receive your credit report you also receive a dispute form that you may fill out, marking appropriate boxes and giving a brief explanation. This method may be just as effective in instances; we have found that a drafted letter gives more room for the consumer to convey their grievances. It also seems to get more respect due to the effort of having to write the letter.)

It may seem that this advice is ridiculous or outrageous, but I guarantee you that this is the **LEGAL** process practiced by professionals. You are guaranteed the right to dispute all information you feel to be erroneous, or not totally precise under **The Fair Credit Reporting Act.** **The Fair Credit Billing Act** relinquishes you from the responsibility of paying for questionable billing errors and defective goods or services. I must reemphasize that I am not suggesting that you avoid paying legitimate debts. But, if you feel there is a possible error with an account you <u>still owe</u> (closed or open), it's definitely within the your rights to **DISPUTE IT!** So, if one of your open accounts indicates that you have not been paying on time (**late pays**), and *<u>you feel</u>* their records may be off a few days, you know what to do, **DISPUTE IT**. The idea is to have the credit bureau do the time consuming task of verifying each item disputed or <u>simply</u> removing it. A little note of encouragement to you, in 1991 TRW (now Experian) admitted that approximately **50%** of all their files contained errors! Its up to you DISPUTE, or continue living within the realm of bad credit. The laws were created for a reason, so use them to your advantage.

Before I give you some items below that are worth disputing, I would like to give you some tactics and facts that will help you dispute items and get them off of your credit reports. First, when disputing any item on a credit report you must appear professional to the credit bureaus. I told you that this process will take time and patience, and I recommend that you practice it. Keep in mind that the people handling your requests are just like you and me. So, if your courteous in your letters, and use creative variations of the sample dispute phrases provided in the next section of this kit, you may avoid the credit bureau checking every item you dispute. You will also be happy to know that when items are removed from your credit report, the original creditor is unaware that the items have been removed.

You know by now that there are three separate credit bureaus. You may encounter situations where only one of the credit bureaus is able to verify a disputed item. If this is the case, simply wait a couple of months and dispute it again. When you go over your credit reports and identify an item that you feel should be removed, be sure to check the date that it was _last reported_. If the item was recently reported to the credit bureau, you should wait a couple of months before disputing. Recall, that information is considered outdated after **60** days. Another reason is that the credit bureau may not consider your request legitimate if the item was just reported last month. What ever you do, don't add threats of any nature to your dispute phrases and always consider even the smallest error as significant. You will be astonished with what you can accomplish with this kit if you are patient and diligent. Remember, the credit bureaus don't have anything to do with the condition of your credit history. Their job is simply to sell and gather information on you. It's your job to ensure that the information is absolutely correct, or live with the consequences.

Here are a few, definitely not all, items that you should dispute:

-ALL ERRONEOUS ITEMS ON YOUR REPORT!

-IF THERE IS ANY INFORMATION THAT DOES NOT BELONG TO YOU, ESPECIALLY IF THE SOCIAL SECURITY NUMBER LISTED IS NOT YOURS!

-If the account amount or outstanding balance is wrong.

-If any account date may be wrong (date of last activity, date opened, date closed, highest amount owed).

-If you disagree with the amount of days that a payment is late (30, 60, 90 days).

-If your name is spelled wrong or there is a previous marital name no longer used.

-If you think the account # is wrong.

-If you never had a felony conviction.

-If you disagree with a ex-employer being listed on your report.

-If you disagree with any aspect of a bankruptcy, foreclosure, repossession, tax lien (date filed?).

-If you have no knowledge or disagree that a collection agency handled your account.

In 1991, TRW (now Experian), admitted in court that approximately **50%** of all their files contained errors. I believe an admission that strong gives the consumer ample authority to scrutinize and dispute all questionable items on their credit report!

Search for possible errors.

Specific Credit
Report Items

This section of the kit is a comprehensive overview of the four major information groups contained in each report, i.e. **Personal, Basic Credit, Public Record, and Inquires**. Each group is defined and broken down into specific areas of concern. For instance, you will find Bankruptcy under the Public Records group along with Child Support and Tax Liens. At the end of each specific area you will find a sample phrase that should be used as an example when your letter of dispute is ready to be produced. You must keep in mind that the information contained in this kit is intended for use as a tool in helping you remove information from your credit report that may be erroneous, outdated, or what you believe to be improperly recorded. The kit is not designed as a legal reference for the laws governing any court proceedings. It's a tool for assisting you in understanding how the credit system works and your rights in resolving your credit history dilemmas. The kit does not provide any legal definitions or advice when it comes to court affiliated credit problems. But, you will find advice on handling these types of credit problems once it becomes a matter of being recorded information in your credit history. Also, it is important to keep in mind that some Basic Credit information can become a matter of Public Record once a Civil Judgment or Lien is placed against your wages or taxes. For this reason you may have look for an item that you have questions about under the topic of Basic Credit and not Public Record, or vise-versa.

Note: You may a add a note than is no more than **100 words** in length explaining any circumstances that may be associated to the current status of any item. This request should be included with your dispute letter that is located in the appendix. I don't recommend that you do this unless ALL attempts of disputing have failed. In other words, if there is a legitimate negative item that cannot be resolved by disputing, you can add a positive comment beneath it in hope that a potential creditor evaluating your report will take your note into consideration.

There are four major groups of information on your credit report-Personal, Basic Credit, Public Record, and Inquiries. All areas should be very closely scrutinized for any questionable errors.

Specific Credit Issues

"Is it really necessary that a potential creditor knows how many times you were married and where you lived ten years ago?"

PERSONAL SECTION:

The personal section is simply the section of the credit report that contains the basic personal facts about you: your legal name, your social security no., birth date, where you live, and who work for. The location of this information is on your credit report depends on the credit bureau that you are dealing with. For instance, Trans Union will locate all of your personal information at the top of the very first page. Where as Equifax, will locate the information at the beginning and near the end of the report. Each credit bureau uses a different information format. You will be happy to know that this is the section that is the easiest to rectify. On the other hand, it is also the section that seems to collect the most **NON-ESSENTIAL** information that should be removed.

By non-essential, I mean the personal information that really isn't pertinent to your credit integrity, outdated or no longer true. Is it really necessary that a creditor or mortgage company know how many times you were married and where you lived ten years ago? This type of information is not relevant to your credit standing. Besides, if somebody truly desires to know this information, you would be the best qualified to answer their question personally, and not some past creditor!

Many find it very surprising to learn that **THEY** are the leading supplier of non-essential information to the credit bureaus. Unaware how things work, you either divulged your current personal status in order to obtain credit some where, or you had an account turned over to a collection agency which took time to investigate your current whereabouts and status. My point is you have probably collected a lot of irrelevant information on your report which makes it appear **bad** to potential creditors. Unlike the other sections of your credit report, your personal section **DOES NOT** have any time restraints. In other words, the only way personal information is updated is by *you* supplying the credit bureau with the most recent and correct information. And the only way to get rid of all the other non-essential information is by *you* taking control and telling them to **remove it**. Your report should **only** reflect the most current and accurate personal information!

Most people have all of this non-essential information on their credit report not knowing that you had the power to remove it all along. **Women** tend to lug around more useless information in the personal section of their report than men. It has something to do with getting married and all of the joyous ramifications that go with it, like changing your name on every important document. If you happen to be a lady who has had this pleasure more than once, you may find relief in knowing that you can now rid yourself of all that non-essential personal information that has been plaguing you. In all seriousness, it is totally within the realms of the law, to remove this type of information. You can't remove everything from this section or alter your social security number, so don't bother trying. You will only draw unnecessary and undesired attention to yourself. The items that must stay on your credit report, as stated in the law, are your legal name, social security #, birthdate, current address and employer. **The credit bureaus can only maintain information that is believed to be actual and current.** You have the right to enhance your credit report so that it indicates your credit history as best possible. It is your right to remove all information that is erroneous, obsolete, outdated, or has no pertinence to your credit integrity!

Most people will not have difficulty disputing items in this section, as long as your requests are not outrageous. Although the law states that they have to, it just doesn't seem possible, nor cost effective, for the credit bureaus to try and verify these types of disputes. Another reason is that they don't have the means nor desire to verify a former address, spouse, or employer. After all, who knows better than you, what personal information belongs and what doesn't, **RIGHT**! If by some coincidence they do have documentation, which verifies a disputed item, they must by law disclose it to you. You then have the right to dispute the validity of the document. Why tie up a lot of time and money over an incorrect address or employer, just remove it and clean your hands. After all, this is your personal information contained in this report. It is your right to make sure that this information is current and accurate! Any item that may reflect bad upon you should be removed.

You have the right to enhance your credit report so that it indicates your credit history as best as possible. It is your right to remove all information that is erroneous, obsolete, outdated, or has no pertinence to your credit integrity!

Keep it personal

"Many people hastily sign things before they fully understand what they are signing, especially if there is a free gift involved."

<u>Here are a few sample phrases for disputing bad information:</u>

<u>Former employer</u>: " The previous employer indicated on my credit report is not correct, please remove it from my file."

<u>If former spouse is listed</u>: " I am not married. This is incorrect, please remove it."

<u>Former name or A.K.A.</u>: " The name recorded on my credit report is incorrect, please remove it from my file."

<u>Former addresses</u>: " The addresses noted are not correct, please remove them." (You should only have the past 2-5 years reflected on your credit report.)

Note: Any information that may reflect you negatively to any future recipient of your credit report should be removed!

"This item recorded in my file is incorrect, please remove it."

INQUIRIES:

Inquiries are the result of somebody viewing your credit history. They will appear toward the end of your credit report, and are indicated in such a way that they are easily distinguished. Experian for instance, will locate your inquiries at the end of the report under the heading, Your Credit Was Reviewed By: Experian also tells you that the following items are inquiries. Each inquiry list *who* looked at your report, *when*, **a number** they may have assigned to you, and perhaps the *reason of the inquiry*. If a subscriber code no. is given, instead of the actual name of the inquirer, a call to the credit bureau is necessary. Simply give the credit bureau the subscriber code and ask them to identify who it is.

Many people hastily sign things before they fully understand what they are signing, especially if there is a free gift involved. Often when people receive their credit reports for the first time they are astonished by a huge list of inquiries on their report. This astonishment quickly turns into anger after they are unable to recall when they gave permission for all of these companies to view their credit history. The immediate reaction of a lot of people is that they have fallen victim to fraud. Actually they are the ones responsible for allowing this to happen by not paying close attention to what they are signing. Once you sign a release authorizing permission to view your credit, you automatically add an inquiry to your credit report. Permission is sometimes given without you realizing what you have done.

Specific Credit Report Items

Creditors or prospective parties, such as LANDLORDS or perhaps a future employer, usually have you sign a release, which allows them access to your credit history. This release is usually nestled within a bunch of fine print that most people don't bother reading thoroughly. Once you have signed this, they have the right to make a judgment about you based on their findings. Most parties whom you will be dealing with are quite open about doing a credit check. If you choose to decline access to them, they have the <u>right</u> to refuse business with you. It's a catch-22 situation. If you have problems with your credit, you lose. Something else to keep in mind, collection agencies that take over your accounts, are legally allowed access to your credit history without your permission.

Inquiries on your credit report are not necessarily a bad thing. In fact, most creditors with whom you have a revolving credit account with, such as Visa or MasterCard, do periodic checks on your credit report to evaluate your current credit standing. If your credit circumstances have changed making you a risk for them, they may choose to close your account, like insurance companies do. These types of actions anger many people, but it's still within their legal rights.

The problem with inquiries is that they remain on your credit reports for a **maximum of two-years**. Each time you apply for credit somewhere another inquiry is added to the list. Thus, within a couple of years, it's quite possible that you can accumulate quite a few inquiries if you are not careful. A problem develops when you have an unusual amount of inquiries within this two year time frame. What happens is the next person who takes a look at your credit report becomes curious about why there are so many inquiries on your report that do not match your open credit accounts. This scenario makes it appear that you have been applying for credit everywhere and for some reason you are being denied credit. In a nutshell, too many inquiries draw undesired attention. Point systems, such as Mavis Beacon, will consider an above average number of inquires as points against a favorable score. Switch places with a prospective creditor for a minute. Wouldn't you be a little suspicious if below a questionable credit history you see a sizable list of businesses that for some reason have denied this person credit? I don't know about you, but hesitation is the first thing that comes into my mind. A real quick way to get a whole bunch of inquiries is to try and finance a car. Ten inquiries may appear overnight if a car dealer or two is shopping around for a finance company that will take your account, so beware!

You should not allow yourself to obtain more than six inquiries at any given time. This practice can help you avoid unnecessary attention. Dispute inquiries off of your credit report as you would any other item. Use **figure 5** in the appendix.

Inquiries are a common part of credit reporting. The problem arises when to many inquires are listed in a short period of time drawing undesired attention. Basically, to many inquires reflect as a negative mark on your credit report, get rid of them!

Inquiry

"Always remember the golden rule,

NEVER NEVER NEVER,

deal with a collection agency."

<u>Here are a few sample phrases for disputing inquiries:</u>

"The inquiry accounts listed (or Hi-lighted) do not belong to me, please remove them."

"I never applied for credit here, please remove it from my file."

"This inquiry is more than two years old, please remove it from my file."

"The inquiry listed is not correct, please remove it at once."

BASIC CREDIT:

CATEGORY (1) ACCOUNTS:

Basic credit can be broken down into two simple categories. The first category encompasses all of your credit accounts that are considered desirable and righteous such as **Bank Credit Cards (Visa, MasterCard, American Express), Department Store Accounts, Automobile or Home Loans or any type of Bank Loan or Mortgages**. These types of accounts are similar in that they all possess an Interest Rate Factor on any outstanding balance amounts. Most of these types of accounts are revolving and make up a large percentage of your ongoing credit history. It should be your goal to have **only these types of accounts** reflected on your credit reports with a good standing rating. As far as credit is concerned, these are your meat and potato accounts that fatten up your credit integrity. You must try and keep these accounts free of derogatory remarks. These remarks come in the form of your payment performance. If you have **Late or Slow payments** noted along with these lines of credit, you should Dispute their validity and have them removed. You want these accounts to reflect that you are a very responsible person. **Any comments that are anything but positive should be REMOVED.**

If one of these accounts has already hit rock bottom and has either been turned over to the In House Collections Department, or even worse a collection agency, then **Disputing** the complete accuracy of this account is necessary. Everybody falls upon hard times at some point or another, but you shouldn't have to live with this type of indignity for seven years. If you are now rebuilding your credit integrity after a period of financial hardship, you may still have derogatory accounts listed on your report that hinder your progress. If these accounts have been paid off and closed, you should have them **removed**. If after several attempts of Disputing these accounts, you are still unsuccessful at getting them removed, your next alternative is having the memos associated with these accounts changed. For instance, you may have a memo like *'PD COLL ACCT'* changed to *'PAID STATUS'. SECTION 5* of the kit details how you can compromise a deal with your creditors.

Always remember the golden rule, **NEVER NEVER NEVER**, deal with a _collection agency_. The **LAW** clearly states that you don't have to deal with them unless you agree to. See the section on debt collectors to learn more about this. Information provided within this Book will explain in detail how you handle them. As stated before, I am not suggesting that you try and evade payment for services and/or merchandise rendered, but merely suggesting that there is a better way to handle these types of accounts.

CATEGORY (2) ACCOUNTS:

The second category encompasses all of those accounts that seem to have only one intent, **REVENGE** against you. Examples of these accounts are: **LANDLORD, Medical (ambulance fees, x-rays, dental, etc..), Rental Centers, Phone Co. or Utilities, Public Records (bankruptcies, repossessions, tax liens, etc..) or COLLECTION AGENCIES.** All of these accounts, and I am sure that you can think of a few more, are accounts that you should concentrate on removing. These accounts, or lines of information, on your credit report cause you to be perceived negatively. Especially, when it comes to a prospective creditor and the total amount of points you scored on their point system. Most of the lines of information were placed on your credit report as a revenge or scare tactic to force you to pay. You'll be happy to learn that you shouldn't encounter a great deal of trouble when **Disputing** these types of accounts with the exception of some public records that take a little more patience and work. The reason: companies or persons who practice this are not equipped to handle the verification process. Recall, if they cannot produce adequate verification within 30 days, they have to remove that line of information by law. For this reason, a lot of you will encounter success with your first attempt. But if you don't, and they come back as being verified, wait the sufficient amount of time, about 60 days, and dispute it again. If you are persistent enough with your disputes, you will find success. Be sure and remove all lines of information that are beyond the allotted seven year period.

If you are currently being harassed by a credit collector for any credit matter, refer to the section on debt collectors immediately, and take appropriate actions to stop them

Collection Agencies

> *"Nine times out of ten, not even the medical billing department can adequately explain their legitimacy."*

If the bill isn't paid within this impossible time frame, it will be turned over to a collection agency.

Here are a few sample phrases for disputing these accounts:

"The last date of payment is incorrect (or amount of days late), please remove or correct."

"I have no recollection of this account belonging to me (closed acct., utility, medical, rental), please remove it from your records."

"Responsibility of this account does not belong to me, as verification will prove. Please remove this item at once."

"The outstanding balance indicated is incorrect. Either correct this error or remove the item entirely."

"The information provided by Mr. Landlord is not at all accurate or true, please remove this item at once."

"I have no knowledge of this item (tax lien, foreclosure, repossession, etc..). This information is very damaging to my credit integrity and must be removed at once."

"The item indicated is outdated and no longer correct, please remove it from my file."

MEDICAL ACCOUNTS:

These are accounts that are associated with your basic credit, but I chose to add a section on them just because of the many credit injustices they enact on the unaware. Lets face it, everybody needs insurance because of the high expense of medical treatment. But many of us, including myself, are unclear at times about the exact coverage that is offered by the insurance. Not only that, many of us are unsure of the billing practices that go along with a hospital visit or stay.

Even though they wont admit it, hospitals have the irreparable tendency to overcharge for their services. I can't count the times I have been told the same scenario about itemized hospital expenses and their collage of confusing codes. Nine times out of ten, not even the medical billing department can adequately explain their legitimacy. They just seem to give the same answer time and time again, " all of the supplies used to treat you were unmistakably counted, measured, weighed and documented. If the bill isn't paid within this impossible time frame, it will be turned over to a collection agency." Maybe it's just me, but I have a problem with anybody who claims that they are perfect and find it impossible that may have miscounted a cotton swab or two during a nine hour surgery. It seems that the only way that continual errors of this nature are brought to light, and acknowledgment that there may be a problem, is when a major news program like *'20/20'* is brought in to investigate such types of <u>justified CRIME</u>, like **Bill Shifting**.

These programs have such enormous power and money that they can't be ignored and shoved underneath the carpet like they do to you and me. It sure is funny how they will adamantly deny all allegations until they are presented with all of the evidence. Even then, they claim it to be an isolated incident that is very rare. The fact is, there are countless errors made on their part everyday. And people like you and me don't have the resources to fight them! Only those very persistent people, or those who may have a medical or legal background, have any idea of what is legal and what isn't when it comes to being billed.

If you have ever had the unfortunate experience of having to be taken in an ambulance and treated in emergency, you probably found out that your two mile trip cost around $400-$500. The fun doesn't stop there, you are then slapped with what it seems like a bill for everybody who looked or touched you in the emergency room. If you are kept overnight and treated by any additional doctors, besides the emergency resident, you will receive their bills as well. Heaven forbid if they give you a Band-Aid and forget to charge you the absolutely preposterous cost of $5.00. I'm sorry, I can't stand the ridiculous itemized billing system they use. I in no way feel I am cheating them if I refuse to pay for some of the materials used to treat me that they buy for $20 and charge me $300. Half the time all of the separate items they list are part of a kit they already have listed. I hate their billing system that diverts the losses from an inept individual, who can't afford their services, to the costs of another, who supposedly has the so-called 'means' to afford it. I encourage you to **DISPUTE** any and all charges that you feel to be **bogus, unjust or unapproved**. That's right, a lot of times you are charged with items and/or services that neither you, nor any other family member, agreed to receive. This isn't legal and by law has to be removed from your credit report.

Here are a few sample phrases for disputing these accounts:

"This item was covered by insurance as verification will prove. Please remove at once."

"I never consented or asked for this service. This bill is incorrect, please remove."

"I was never transported in an ambulance, please remove this from my credit report."

"I never received this item or service, please remove it at once."

There is some good news. Once the defaulted loan is paid in full the defaulted status is automatically removed and replaced with a paid in full status as if it never was in default.

Student Loans

35

"Credit collectors especially love these accounts because of their government affiliation. This type of account offers to them a variety of intimidating ploys to convince you to pay them the original amount and up to 44% in collection fees."

This is legal only if you have signed their papers or forms agreeing to their terms.

"The account indicated is outdated and no longer correct, please remove it from my file."

STUDENT LOANS:

The Federal Government as you know backs student loans, sometimes referred to as Stafford Loans. Whenever Uncle Sam is involved in placing a line of information against your credit, as in a defaulted Stafford Loan, you will more than likely be unable to avoid it. Unless there are legitimate errors associated with what is represented on your credit report, I suggest you chose an alternate means of correcting this problem. If you disagree with the balance owed, the account number, or if the loan doesn't even belong to you, by all means **Dispute** it. Don't let me discourage you from trying to dispute this type of item, but seriously consider using SECTION 5 of this kit to work out a deal if necessary. Your social security number is most likely your account number as well. For this reason, it can be difficult in avoiding the legitimacy of this item.

The same laws govern a defaulted student loan as any other credit account on your credit report. With this in mind, recall the seven-year cycle. If you have been living with a defaulted loan for a significant period of time, as a derogatory line of credit, what ever you do, consider this fact. If you start repayment NOW, you will only be **restarting** the seven-year period that it is allowed to be on your credit report. Repayment may be the noble thing to do, but also consider the credit anguish that you have been experiencing because of its presence. If you begin repayment, you are only extending this torture.

If a credit collector because of a defaulted loan is currently harassing you, refer to the section on debt collectors immediately, and take appropriate actions to stop them. Credit collectors especially love these accounts because of their government affiliation. This type of account offers to them a variety of intimidating ploys to convince you to pay them the original amount and up to 44% in collection fees. This is legal only if you have signed their papers or forms agreeing to their terms.

You have to be very careful because these collection agencies are very clever. A trick they often use is to form their letters to closely resemble those of official government offices. Just to be on the safe side, always respond to them with a certified letter requesting copies of the original loan documentation that bears your signature. Also request details of all charges and fees. By doing this, you will immediately determine if this is official or simply a collection agency, whom you should **NEVER** deal with. If this is official, you can either try and dispute it or refer to the section on compromising with a creditor, and see if a compromise is possible. If you do choose to deal with the defaulted loan, most of the time the Defaulted Student Loan Office will usually be very cooperative in working out a deal with you, if they feel you are sincere. They have several different payment programs to fit the needs of everybody. There is some good news. Once the defaulted loan is paid in full the defaulted status is automatically removed and replaced with a paid in full status as if it never was in default.

Also, be aware that the Student Loan Department, with Federal Government backing, has the right to seize your tax refunds as well as garnish your wages. For these reasons, I suggest you work out an agreement and avoid the humiliation of any further legal actions.

Here are a few sample phrases for disputing inaccurate student loans:

"This loan is not mine. Please compare s.s.# and remove it from my credit report."

"The balance indicated is erroneous. Please correct or remove this item entirely."

"The account #/social security # indicated with this loan is not mine, please remove it."

"This loan has been paid in full. Please remove all derogatory information from this item."

"The loan indicated is outdated and no longer correct, please remove it from my file."

PUBLIC RECORDS:

If you have items under the Public Record section of your credit report, you are probably fully aware of it. Items of Public Record are always court affiliated. You may or may not of had an attorney involved in your particular situation, but either way, I am sure that you can recall the circumstances that lead you to court i.e. (repossession, bankruptcy, foreclosure, etc.). Under the **Fair Credit Reporting Act**, any Public Record (documented public information or court proceedings) that may affect your current credit standing can be placed on your credit report. The purpose behind placing Public Records on your credit report is so any prospective creditor, or interested party, can be readily provided with a means of measuring your character and/or credit worthiness. Some examples of Public Record are as follows: Bankruptcies, Child Support, Civil Judgments, Divorces, Felony Convictions, Foreclosures, Repossessions, State or Federal Tax Liens, Wage Garnishments.

Public Record items should be handled in exactly the same manner that you handle any other line of credit on your credit report, by disputing any believed inaccuracy including a comment to remove the item entirely.

What are your legal rights?

"An unexpected death in the family, or some other uncontrolable circumstance may force an individual or family to file for bankruptcy."

There are four types of Bankruptcies, Chapters 7,11,12, and 13.

Many times items of this nature are the direct result of a bad economy (job loss) or misfortune (death or accident). If this is the case, I am sure you know the helplessness and despair it causes. If that isn't bad enough, you are then forced to live with this indignity for the period of seven to **TEN** years. That's right, a **chapter 7 bankruptcy**, and depending on which state you live in, a civil judgment, can legally be listed on your credit report for **TEN** years. It's as if you are being punished for a crime. But never the less, it's the law.

Public Record items should be handled in exactly the same manner that you handle any other line of credit on your credit report. The same credit laws previously mentioned, govern Public Record items in the same way, except for the items listed above. The problem with Public Record items listed on your credit report is they are very damaging to your credit integrity. Creditors, insurance companies, employers, and so on, tend to judge you pessimistically when they see a Public Record item listed. This predisposed conception of you overflows from your credit standing into your personal integrity. Even though there may be events associated with your circumstances that were of no fault to you, like a vehicular accident, which impaired your ability to work three years ago, people and creditors will tend to judge you without reason. Needless to say, Public Record items can be difficult to remove from your credit report because of their readily available legal documentation. In cases such as bankruptcies, you may have even initiated the proceedings and attested to its validity in court. But then again, the court system doesn't have the time nor the personnel to do every credit bureau verification request, IF ANY.

People and computers often make mistakes. There is nothing illegal about you **DISPUTING** any Public Record item you deem incorrect in any shape or form. Even if you are <u>uncertain</u> whether your case or item of record was handled correctly, it is your right to **dispute it**. Your uncertainty may be the way that this item can be removed. If there is an obvious mistake about an item of this nature, DO NOT hesitate for a minute to **dispute it**. The **only way** that you are going to have a chance at getting a Public Record item off of your credit report is by **DISPUTING IT**. You may have to **DISPUTE** it three or four times. But let me tell you, only the persons who are not shy and that are very persistent are going to be the ones who experience success in this area. Don't think it's impossible because removal of these items happens more than the credit bureau would like to admit. Believe me, I have seen and helped it happen. This may excite you into acting quickly on Public Records is: **once the item is removed it will never return to your credit report**. You shouldn't have to suffer such an indignity for your misfortune. Again, there are always going to be mistakes made by the people recording information on your credit report, but it is up to you to recognize them. As Louis Pasteur stated, *" Chance favors the prepared mind."*

BANKRUPTCY-see entire section on bankruptcy

CHILD SUPPORT, DIVORCE, AND FELONY CONVICTIONS:

In retrospect to the credit laws being revamped, the topics of Child Support, Divorce, and Felony Convictions are very controversial as to whether they should be reflected on your credit report or not. The law states that it is **legal** for all of these items to be placed on your credit report. The biggest dispute against this practice is the question of morality. Judging by the practices of the three credit bureaus, child support and felony convictions are the most debatable. Of the three credit bureaus, only one of them chooses to list child support, **Equifax**. As far as felony convictions, Experian doesn't list any criminal records. Even though a divorce is an item of Public Record, the assertion that it affects personal credit stability is highly questionable. Unless there is a universal agreement between all of the credit bureaus to report something or not, the item of information should be withheld. The decision for one credit bureau to report something and another not to signifies that there may not be a need for it to be reported as an indicator of your credit stability.

I agree that there should be a system established for apprehending dead beat Dads, and reflecting these items on ones credit report may be the answer. What bothers me is that: should the fathers who adhere to their parental obligations suffer the same consequences as those who don't? As it stands now, any father who is court ordered to pay child support is subject to have it reported to the credit bureau. This action can carry with it adverse affects to ones credit standing. Thus, the law will be punishing everyone for the faults of a few, which is unconstitutional. The second question that arises is, if this is such a good system, why isn't everyone using it. Until these questions can be resolved, and an impartial system established, items of this nature should not be representational of ones credit integrity.

This little fact may excite you into acting quickly on Public Record items: **once a public record item is removed, it can never be put back onto your credit report**

"Judging by the practices of the three credit bureaus, child support and felony convictions are the most debatable. Of the three credit bureaus, only one of them chooses to list child support, Equifax."

Although divorce is a personal matter, and I believe it should be kept that way, it is handled through the courts and therefore becomes a matter of Public Record. As far as I am concerned, and most of you that I deal with agree, divorce should have no bearing on their credit stability. In most instances the only way a divorce, or even a marriage in this case, gets reported to the credit bureau is by you telling them. There are some messy divorces that do directly affect ones credit. But for the most part, the credit bureaus wouldn't know if you were married or not, if you didn't tell them. There is nothing in the law that states that you have to indicate if you are 'MARRIED'. Many of you may feel as I do, and reserve the right NOT to list this type of information. I believe it is one of those things that if somebody desires that information, let them ask me directly. There is no need for them to refer to my credit history to see if I am married. Many of you ladies out there may even feel unsafe if somebody was to find out that you were not married and lived alone. A divorce is not necessarily pertinent to your credit integrity and should be removed from your credit report.

As far as **felonies** are concerned, your credit history isn't part of Hawthorn's *The Scarlet letter*, where you should be forced to wear the letter 'F' for the world to see. Your criminal history is just that, your criminal history. If somebody needs this type of information, let them order a copy of your police record, not your credit history. You should have any items of this nature removed by disputing their legitimacy.

Here are a few sample phrases for disputing these items:

"The item (child support) listed does not belong to me, please remove it."

"I was never convicted of a felony or any other crime, please remove at once."

"I am not divorced, or was never married, please remove this from your records."

REPOSSESSIONS, FORECLOSURES, & CIVIL JUDGMENTS:

If you have experienced any one of these situations, you were probably not surprised to find it on your credit report. Many people are under the false assumption that if you voluntarily surrender a vehicle or home, that it will not be reflected on your credit. Even when a person drives the vehicle back to place of purchase and hands them the keys, this is considered a **Voluntary Repossession**. The law states that if you purchase or lease a vehicle, *and for whatever the reason*, it has to be returned (repossessed in the night or voluntarily surrendered) because of non-payment, you are still obligated to pay the remaining balance. Even if the car is stolen and never seen again, or quits running the day after the warranty expires, you are still responsible. This is quite upsetting for many people. But, if you had taken the time, or even asked the dealer to explain some of the legal jargon that is so nicely worded in the purchase agreement, you would have discovered this binding clause. Once it gets to this stage, you have violated the terms of the contract and will probably find yourself being bombarded by credit collectors, or in court fighting a **Civil Suit**. The same principle applies to the purchase of homes.

Many people purchase a home, encounter unforeseen problems, and then come to the conclusion that they can't afford it any more. At this point, many of the homeowners figure they will just take the loss and file 'A Deed In Due Of'. What they are not aware of is this is still considered a **Foreclosure**, and will be reflected on your credit report as such. Nobody cares about the circumstances surrounding your actions; they simply want their money. If they don't get their money, they will without hesitation take you to court. Whether they get their money or not is up to you. Circumstances of this nature usually result with the homeowner filing Bankruptcy to avoid any further criminal actions. Once this action is taken, the mortgage company will do its best to retaliate by reporting all derogatory information to the credit bureaus. Revenge is usually the motive behind many of these types of credit problems. If they can make it a little more difficult on you, believe me they will. It's as if the situations surrounding the problem in the first place weren't hot enough, they just had to add a little more gas to the fire.

If there is a good side to foreclosures and repossessions, it has to be that they can only exist on your credit report for **seven** years. Both of these items, like any other derogatory line of credit, are governed by the **seven year cycle** and *The Fair Credit Reporting Act,* which entitles you to **dispute their accuracy**. As I have stated time and time again, the only way to remove these types of items is by scrutinizing every aspect of them, and **disputing** everything in question. Besides a Bankruptcy, the only thing worse than these two items is a **Civil Judgment**.

*As far as **felonies** are concerned, your credit history isn't part of Hawthorn's The Scarlet letter, where you should be forced to wear the letter 'F' for the world to see.*

Criminal Hisory & Credit

"The law states that if you purchase or lease a vehicle, and for what ever the reason, it has to be returned (repossessed in the night or voluntarily surrendered) because of non-payment, you are still obligated to pay the remaining balance."

Many times that unyielding revenge that I just mentioned will come out in the form of a civil judgment. A civil judgment may be the result of a creditors ultimate revenge against you. If a creditor feels an adequate resolution cannot be made, they may choose to drag you through court. An example that may cause such uncontrollable malice may be a court ordered vehicle surrendering that never results with the vehicle being returned. In a case such as this, a creditor has the right to sue you, and have a civil judgment placed against your credit. To make a long story short, a **civil judgment** can legally be placed against your credit for **TEN** years. After the ten years expire, the creditor has the option of renewing the civil judgment for an additional **TEN years**. So actually, a civil judgment can be held against your credit for **TWENTY years**. A civil judgment is in no way limited to repossessions. The IRS is very familiar with this tool. I hope that you fully understand the gravity of these types of credit situations, and take upon yourself to **DISPUTE** every questionable part of each item. The only way to get these types of items removed is by exercising your right to **DISPUTE ANY ITEM THAT YOU FEEL ISN'T ACCURATE.**

Here are a few sample phrases for disputing these items:

"I never had a vehicle repossessed on this date, please remove this item."

"I know nothing about a civil judgment in this amount, please remove it from my file."

"The foreclosure item listed is not correct. Please remove this item from my report."

"The item indicated is outdated and no longer correct, please remove it from my records."

S E C T I O N   F O U R

THE IRS, TAX LIENS, & WAGE GARNISHMENTS:

Even the acronyms IRS, bring chills to many. Contrary to popular belief, the IRS is able and willing to work out repayment arrangements that will satisfy both of you. It is true that the IRS has the means to **garnish your wages**, **seize your bank account**, and place **tax** liens against you if necessary. But these actions can all be avoided with one phone call. The IRS can be very aggressive, but they can also be very cooperative and sensitive to a struggling persons needs. It is my recommendation, if you are trying to avoid the IRS that you quit running and try and work out a deal with them. As hard as you may wish, the IRS just isn't going to forget about you. In fact, if you haven't been filing taxes because your afraid of what they will do to you once they catch you, you are simply making your problems worse. **There are no time limitations** for the IRS when trying to collect back taxes. In other words, if you owe for taxes and you decide to leave the earth for twenty years, then return and safely go back to work, your mistaken. You can bet that you wont see a bit of your check once your employer notifies them that you are under employment with them. The IRS has only one limitation, they must resolve any disputes with your tax returns within **three years**, or forget about it. This obviously applies only to those who file.

Many of you also have the false assumption that if you haven't filed in years, that they are going to lock you up and throw away the key once they find you. This is not the case with the IRS. They DON'T lock anybody up for *not filing*. Other offenses like felony tax evasion, will get you a stay in Federal prison, but not because you didn't file. Actually, the IRS has forms that are readily available to you if you are currently under a wage garnishment and desire to work out a repayment plan in order to lift the garnishment. The IRS is always going to be around, and unless you want to file Bankruptcy, you need to give them a call. You can always attempt a dispute to remove a **TAX LIEN** or **GARNISHMENT** from your credit report, but it will probably fail and this is not any way going to alleviate your debt with the IRS. The only way to this one is by either working it out with the IRS or file for a bankruptcy. Don't worry; they don't trace their calls. There are phone numbers to the IRS provided in the appendix of the book.

Take a civil judgement very seriously. They are the only items that can actually be placed on your credit report for a period of 20 years. First 10 years just like a bankruptcy and then an additional ten years if the creditor so chooses.

Civil Judgement

"It is true that the IRS has the means to garnish your wages, seize your bank account, and place tax liens against you if necessary.

But these actions can all be avoided with one phone call to IRS at 1-800-653-9529"

Here are a few sample phrases for disputing IRS problems:

"The tax problem (lien, garnishment, etc.) listed is totally erroneous and must be removed at once."

"I never experienced this item (tax problem) and find it erroneous to be located on my credit file, please remove it from your records as soon as possible."

"The garnishment listed does not belong to me. This item is detrimental to my credit worthiness. Please remove it from my file immediately."

The IRS

Understanding Bankruptcy

Understanding Bankruptcy

If you are reading this section then you may be experiencing or contemplating, what can be one of the most trying points in your life. A bankruptcy can either be one of the greatest set backs in your life financially, or a blessing from the overwhelming stresses of an unanticipated situation, like a permanent loss to a wage earning family member. Either way, a bankruptcy is the absolute worst thing that you can do for your credit rating. There are three types of Bankruptcies in which an individual consumer can file a Chapter 7, 12 or 13. A Chapter 12 bankruptcy is recommended for farmers and their family-debt related problems. Normally, this type of bankruptcy does not apply to the average consumer, and if it does it is more complicated than other bankruptcy options. Therefore, I will not discuss its respective advantages and disadvantages. However, Chapter 7 and Chapter 13 bankruptcies are readily available to most individuals. Unfortunately, these two types of *bankruptcies were at an all time high in 1997, with a record 1.3 million cases being filed*. The reason for my disappointment is a bankruptcy is a truly devastating situation, and I feel for those who must endure such a setback. If at all possible a bankruptcy should be avoided at all cost. The amount of bankruptcies filed in court last year has received the attention of many lawmakers who believe that the system, which was put into place to protect individuals with dire situations, is being outlandishly abused. Some families find that their particular situation deems it absolutely necessary that they file a bankruptcy. While other situations, nonetheless discouraging and frustrating are very much reconcilable with time, better money management, and in some cases professional assistance. It is the reconcilable types of cases that are being filed that are the cause for all of the attention that is being drawn to reform the current system. The changes will come in the form of stringent requirements that will force the consumer to prove that a bankruptcy is absolutely the only alternative and not just a desired plan for eluding just debt. But for now, it is still up to the individual to decide whether a bankruptcy is desired. I must express that a bankruptcy should only be considered as a last resort effort to rectify a financial situation. A bankruptcy is basically committing financial suicide that will have lasting effects even beyond the 10-year statue.

If you have a choice between a chapter 7 and 13 bankruptcy, and a home or other piece of prime property is not involved, **your first choice should be a chapter 7**. I say this because a Chapter 7 totally discharges all of the accounts included in the Bankruptcy, and allows the recovery period to begin. On the other hand, a Chapter 13 Bankruptcy (Wage Earner Plan) sets up a repayment plan for your debts that extends the whole ordeal an additional 3-5 years. In the end, you are still left with a Bankruptcy and devastated credit. At least with a chapter 7, the road to recovery begins immediately. With a Chapter 13, you can burn all of your money for 3-5 years and achieve the same results as someone who filed a Chapter 7 with the exception of a few additional years. The differences are discussed below. If it is truly necessary,

Deciding to file bankruptcy can be one of the most difficult decisions in your life. If you are forced to make this decision, then I recommend you call our affiliate law firm -

Hopp & Flesch
(303) 806-8886

for the finest representation in matters of this nature. Tell them where you got this number and receive a FREE initial consultation.

Finding the road to recovery

If your in a real clincher

with your credit issues, and

wish to speak with a legal

professional about having

your credit

problems resolved for you,

then I recommend you

contact our affiliates:

Lexington law Firm

1-800-653-9529

Tell them where you got this

number and receive a

FREE 30 minute

consultation with

an attorney specializing

in credit!

then the question becomes which Chapter is best suited for your particular situation. And **DO NOT** forget that this book will become an invaluable resource for starting over and rebuilding your credit situation. Whether you choose to continue your financial battles or believe that the situation has far exceeded your capabilities financially, with your health and security becoming an issue, this credit resource will help you even resolve the aftermath of a bankruptcy. This overview is not intended as legal advice that can be applied to every situation for every individual. If you have specific questions that are not covered in this overview we recommend you call **Hopp & Flesch for bankruptcy** questions and **Lexington Law firm** for help with resolving **all other credit report issues.**

Chapter 7 bankruptcies occur most frequently and by far are the easiest to prepare and complete. Individuals who prepare their own Petition and Schedules may want to consider legal counsel. But, this particular chapter of bankruptcy is performed on a regular basis without an attorney because of its strait forward layout. An individual can use the attached forms in the appendix of this book as an entire mock bankruptcy. I say mock because it would be a really fat book to include the forms for every state in nation, since each state has its own variations of forms. Nonetheless, you can go through the provided forms filling out everything pertinent to your situation, gathering all required information, as if it were your state. By doing this prior to obtaining the actual forms for your state you will discover exactly where you will need help in filling out the forms. Mark the areas that you have questions about and fill out the rest. You can then ask the appropriate questions and make performing the chapter 7 bankruptcy yourself, a smooth and easy process. The key things to remember are: **1)** Fill out the provided forms as best as possible, **2)** Note any and all areas that confuse you or that you may question as being applicable to your particular situation. **3)** Prepare a list of questions if necessary, **4)** After completing your forms for your state make sure that the forms have been thoroughly reviewed for completeness before submitting, so you don't encounter any delays. I must warn you that there are possible civil and criminal penalties for not bringing a bankruptcy in good faith or falsifying your financial condition, within the schedules.

A **Chapter 7 discharge will release almost all unsecured debts except for the following: 1)** most state and federal taxes; **2)** Any indebtedness caused by fraud; **3)** Debts for alimony, maintenance, child support and other divorce related debts; **4)** Debts for intentional or malicious injury to a person or property; **5)** criminal fines and/or penalties; **6)** Educational loans; and **7)** Debts that could have been listed on a previous bankruptcy.

The important thing to remember about a Chapter 7 bankruptcy is that *you can pick and choose those creditors* (those people or entities you owe money to) you wish to repay, as long as you have no assets that are non-exempt. For example, if you have a car loan and you do not wish to keep the car, you may return the vehicle to the loan company and be relieved from paying anything further. In the alternative, if you wish to keep the vehicle you may continue to pay for it and continue to keep it in your possession. Overall, as long as your secured loans (those loans backed by some sort of property such as your car or house) are current, you will find the creditor very agreeable to allow you to keep the security (car or house) and make payments to them as if you hadn't filed bankruptcy. A *Chapter 7 bankruptcy is best suited for those with large unsecured debts*, very few, if any, non-exempt assets and secured debts that are all current at the time of the bankruptcy filing. In other words, it is best for persons who don't own the title to a car and are simply overwhelmed by particular debts such as credit cards, hospital bills, and revolving lines of credit. Especially necessary if you can no longer pay even the minimum amounts due each month on these particular bills, without jeopardizing your welfare or security.

A *Chapter 13 Bankruptcy, on the other hand, is best suited for those individuals who are past due on their home mortgages or other secured loans* and wish to keep the property but cannot bring the loans current immediately. Additionally, anyone contemplating a Chapter 13 bankruptcy must be employed throughout the duration of the action. Basically, a Chapter 13 bankruptcy allows you to repay the amounts past due over a period of from 3 to 5 years, depending upon the circumstances.

The filing of the Chapter 7 and Chapter 13 bankruptcy are almost identical. What makes them different is in the Chapter 13 bankruptcy you must also file a Plan for repayment of the debts you owe. This type of bankruptcy is more complicated and often times more costly based upon the Plan payments and the length of the Plan. Another concern when filing the Plan is whether or not the payments can be made each month as agreed to. If you were to miss as little as one payment, the Plan and the Bankruptcy can be dismissed leaving you in the same position as when you filed to begin with.

Additionally, a Trustee is appointed on each case and she/he receives an additional 10% of any monies paid into the Plan for keeping track of the payments etc. Thus, even if you complete the Chapter 13 on your own, without an attorney, you still will have to pay an additional 10% surcharge on every payment you make. It makes for an expensive alternative to the Chapter 7 bankruptcy. But, for those who are behind on their home mortgage or other secured debts, and do not want their home to be foreclosed or property repossessed, it is the only game in town if a refinance is impossible.

Overall, when contemplating a bankruptcy you must consider your current and future financial conditions. If a bankruptcy is filed today, you may not be able to file again for another 6 to 7 years. Thus, you must consider whether additional debts will be incurred in the future that you will be able to pay or, if not, you may wish to wait to include those debts in your bankruptcy.

RIGHTS AFTER A BANKRUPTCY IS FILED

After you file a bankruptcy, an Automatic Stay occurs which stops most garnishments, foreclosures and other state and federal lawsuits involving the person who has filed. This Automatic Stay may be lifted by the bankruptcy

A Chapter 7 bankruptcy is best suited for those with large unsecured debts, very few, if any, non-exempt assets and secured debts that are all current at the time of the bankruptcy filing

What are my rights?

49

"If anything you see on your credit report seems to be misleading, misreported or remotely inaccurate - Dispute, Dispute, Dispute!!!"

Judge at a creditors request with the Court determining that there is good reason to allow certain actions to proceed. A bankruptcy is often the only way to stop a judgment creditor from further garnishment or attachment, at least in the short term. Many times a **Bankruptcy will allow time to negotiate with the creditor to come to an agreement so the garnishment will be stopped permanently.** Without question, your credit report will see the devastation of filing a bankruptcy. It is very important that you refer to the section on disputing to go through your credit report and clear off any inaccuracies as it pertains to your filing of bankruptcy i.e. duplicates items, multiple listing of the same bankruptcy, inaccurate amounts, accounts, or dates. If you find or believe any little piece of information to be inaccurate in any way you need to dispute that information and tell them to remove the item at once or verify it as being accurate. Remember you can dispute even a bankruptcy and get it removed. I have personally seen it done, so it is not impossible as you are made to believe. If anything you see on your credit report seems to be misleading, misreported or remotely inaccurate - Dispute, Dispute, And Dispute!!!

Whichever Chapter you chose, all of the accounts that were included in the Bankruptcy must adhere to the seven-year cycle. Even though the actual Bankruptcy line is allowed by law to stay on your credit report for the period of **TEN years** from the *date of discharge*, each individual account is dictated by the *date of last activity*. In other words, if you stopped paying on an account two years before you included it in the Bankruptcy, it can only stay on your credit report for an additional five years, regardless of the Bankruptcy. IN FACT, you should inspect these accounts extra carefully for disputable errors as given in the section on disputing. Several different parties have exposed all of these particular accounts to additional handling. In all of this information transferring errors can be very likely. I would guess that more than 50% of the people who have filed a bankruptcy have an error on their report. The typical errors that that appear on the reports: the bankruptcy line appearing more than once (I have seen it appear as many times as 4), a single account that was included in the bankruptcy appearing several times (the most common).

The errors listed above **MUST BE REMOVED**, except for one, and that is on the contingency that it does not contain any errors as well. Now, if outrageous occurrences on your credit report, like a bankruptcy item appearing several times, then it's very possible that there may be other errors such as with the dates and/or amounts, on one of these items. It is **ILLEGAL** for the credit bureaus to maintain errors of this type in your credit report. It is very upsetting that misfortunes of this magnitude occur, as if the circumstances causing you to file a bankruptcy weren't enough! If you're truly blessed with good luck, you may have the pleasure of dealing with five or six accounts on your report appearing multiple times. Seriously, the credit laws clearly state that each account can only be listed error free **ONCE, or REMOVED** altogether. So if this scenario is familiar to you, **DISPUTE ALL OF THEM, IT'S YOUR RIGHT!**

Here are a few sample phrases for disputing Bankruptcy errors:

"The Bankruptcy listed is totally inaccurate, please remove it from my credit report."

"I never filed a Bankruptcy on this date. Please remove this item at once from my file."

"The item listed is a duplicate that was already listed as being included in my Bankruptcy. Please remove this item from my credit report at once."
"The Bankruptcies (accounts) listed do not belong to me, please remove them as indicated."

"The Bankruptcy indicated is outdated and no longer correct, please remove it from my credit report."

Remember you can dispute even a bankruptcy and get it removed. I have personally seen it done, so it is not impossible as you are made to believe. If anything you see on your credit report seems to be misleading, misreported or remotely inaccurate - Dispute, Dispute, Dispute!!!

Watch for errors!

Compromising
With Creditors

Compromising With Creditors

When all attempts at disputing a derogatory line of credit have failed in a successful verification, your next plan of action is to offer a compromise to a creditor. Offering a compromise to a creditor may be difficult, depending on whom you are dealing with, but it is certainly within the law. All of you know what a compromise is, it's an agreement that satisfies both parties involved. In this case the creditor desires, **money**, and you desire a **positive note** attached to your account. The agreement on your part should include the removal of an old memo like '**ACCT IN COLL**', and reflect a desirable memo like '**PAID AS AGREED**'. What the creditor gets in return for this action is a settlement on an outstanding balance that may have, otherwise resulted in a total loss of funds.

When you are ready to make your offer, you must call your creditor and request to speak to someone of authority, not a regular operator. The people answering the phone, who I have nothing against, are merely customer service agents and have no real authority to negotiate the type of deal you require. At this point, you are in a manner of speaking, holding all of the cards, **the money**. Once you give up this money you are in effect giving up your bargaining tool. The money is the key object here. In retrospect to the *seven year cycle*, if you simply send in your money in hopes of clearing an account up, you will be very disappointed to learn that you merely restarted the seven year clock, and that your account will reflect a derogatory memo for the entirety of the seven years. This is why you must put in writing exactly how you want your credit report updated by the creditor. The creditor must receive this compromise letter and agree to it's terms, and sign and return the letter to you before you send any money. You may encounter creditors that claim this type of arrangement is impossible. If this is the case, simply ask to speak to someone of higher authority because they are not telling you the truth. There is nothing illegal about doing this, and **they do** have the authority to report to the credit bureau a simple memo like '**PAID AS AGREED**'. What ever you do, don't give up your bargaining chip (**money**) without getting something in writing that they agree to this compromise.

When you get the right person on the phone and you are able to strike a deal, tell them that you will send in a letter detailing what you have agreed to, and ask them to sign it. Tell them that once this signed agreement is received by you, you will send in your money as agreed. What ever you do, don't be chorused to send in your money based on a verbal promise, because believe it or not, these people may lie to you.

It is in the best interest of a creditor to try and make a deal with you for a partial payment, if not the entire sum, in return for an item either being removed or modified to a positive comment. The alternative is not getting a penny or selling your account to a collection agency.

Legalities of Compromise

The whole purpose of this kit is to show you how to take charge of your credit situation and make things happen. Compromising a settlement is just another technique that is used to help you accomplish your goals.

The whole purpose here is to show you that there are alternative ways to handling bad accounts. You may even ask that they simply strike the whole line from your credit report. The idea is, they have the power to perform such actions, and you now have the knowledge and ability to make actions like this come to life. The whole purpose of this kit is to show you how to take charge of your credit situation and make things happen. Compromising a settlement is just another technique that is used to help you accomplish your goals. There are probably many other ways of rectifying your credit problems, but if you don't expend the energy, you will never see relief from **BAD CREDIT. Figure 7 in the appendix** will give you an example of a compromise letter.

Handling Collection Agencies

The most recent figures estimate that the annual earnings for the Credit Collection Industry are in excess of $70,000,000. I will make it no secret that I do not like credit or debt collectors, and simply will tell you *NEVER TO DEAL WITH THEM.* The **FEDERAL FAIR DEBT COLLECTION PRACTICES ACT** clearly states that you **DO NOT** have to deal with credit or debt collectors. If you would like to see this in writing for yourself, simply write or call your local Federal Trade Commission and request a copy of this law. There you will see that if you take the appropriate actions you can stop these collectors with **ONE** letter. The legal title of this letter is called a **CEASECOMM LETTER** (Cease and Desist). A ceasecomm letter is short for cease communication. Once this letter is received by the credit collection agency, they are forced by law to stop all communication with you, except for one more time to tell you that they will no longer be contacting you, even if the debt is legitimate and you owe money. This means that they **may not** contact you in any way, shape, or form. Not by phone, at work, by fax, by certified mail, by nothing. To good to be true you say, **try it**, and see for yourself.

For all those who have dealt with a credit collection agency or are currently dealing with one, you know how bad they harass you. If you have already made arrangements with a collection agency, and signed their agreements, it is _too late_ for you to send a Ceasecomm Letter. But, if you are currently being harassed and have not agreed to pay them, I recommend you send them a Ceasecomm Letter formatted after Figure 6 in the appendix, immediately. Once the collector contacts you, they are obligated to send you information on the original debtor within five days. Use this information, along with their business information, to fill out your ceasecomm letter. For those who are already stuck with dealing with a credit collector, you will be happy to know that you still have rights.

A credit collector has limitations on the degree to which they can harass you. For instance, they **may not** contact you at work **ever again** if you send them a letter stating that your employer does not approve of their interruptions because it interferes with your work productivity. They *are* allowed to contact you by the communication methods I just mentioned, unless you tell them otherwise. Credit collectors will attempt to reach you by phone at awkward times, like late at night or early in the morning, when they feel they have the best opportunity of catching you at home. By law, unless you inform them otherwise, they cannot contact you by phone before 8:00 A.M. or after 9:00 P.M.. The collector is also prohibited from contacting anybody else but you and your attorney if you happen to have one. Here is a list of other miscellaneous items that a credit collector **CANNOT** do. If they do perpetrate any of these following acts, they are in violation of the law, and you are suggested to contact a reputable attorney in order to file a **Federal Law Suit.**

> " *If you are currently being harassed by a collection agency and have not agreed to pay them, I recommend you send them a Ceasecomm Letter formatted after Figure 6 in the appendix, immediately.* "

Collection Agencies

-They **cannot** make threats against you in any way (personal or property).

-They **cannot** use profane or obscene language when communicating with you.

-If you file a ceasecomm letter, they **cannot** add any remarks to your credit report.

-They **cannot** publish or advertise your debts in any form or fashion.

-They **cannot** falsely imply or impersonate that they are **anyone** else, but the collector.

-They **cannot** distort or exaggerate the amount owed on the account.

-They **cannot** use documentation that gives a false impression of an official Govt. letter.

-They **cannot** threaten to have you arrested.

-Unless they have **already** started proceedings to take these following actions, they cannot threaten to seize your wages, or property. They can exercise these actions if done legally.

Resolving 'BAD' Checks

Most people have at one time or another encountered the problem of exceeding available funds in your checking account causing a check to be returned, or in layman's terms 'bounced.' Most banks will resubmit the check a second time after a day or so to assure that the funds are not available before returning the checks to the creditor or whomever you wrote the check to. At this time you will not only be charged an average returned check fee of $20.00 by your bank, but you will also be charged an additional fee similar to your bank by whomever you wrote the check to. Your failure to keep your checking account records in order by this point has already cost you approximately $40-$50.00. This is just the tip of the iceberg if you don't react and resolve this matter immediately. Besides your bank only tolerating an average of 3-4 incidents of this nature within a 4-month period before closing your account, you now have a collection agency on your back. That's correct; once the check is returned to whomever you wrote it to they usually have a contract with a collection agency that they sell the bad check to in order to minimize the hassle of trying to collect the due funds. This collection agency then tacks on an additional fee and then begins adding outrageous interest to the outstanding amount owed on a daily basis. If your real lucky you may receive a call from the original check bearer before it is turned over to the collection agency to offer you the opportunity to clear this matter up, but usually all of the above happens within a very short time period like a week or so without you even aware that a problem exists.

So you now have a collection agency calling and sending you threatening letters and your asking yourself what do I do??? Your very first step in resolving this matter as quickly and inexpensively as possible is to:

1) <u>Obtain enough money to cover the amount of the check and at least $25.00 extra for the returned check fee</u>. You are about to get a hold of the party that you wrote the check to and try and settle this matter at it's root. By doing this you are cutting out the middleman, the collection agency, and sparing your credit history a derogatory item. You **never ever** want to deal with a collection agency. By paying a collection agency you are automatically agreeing to their conditions, one of which is to have this item recorded in your credit history. Most of the time a collection agency will make you a bunch of empty promises in hope that you will rectify this matter as quickly as possible, promises such as " this will matter will not be put on your credit report if you send all of the money (the amount of the check, collection fees, and interest) right away." Even though this problem began as a returned check you now handle it *exactly* as you would a Debt Collector described in the previous section.

2) <u>Make the call to whomever you wrote the check to</u>. You must have prepared a very good explanation to why this <u>misfortunate incident</u> occurred

A bounced check can get out of control in a very short time period. If you are lucky you will find out about the problem right away. If you immediately contact the party who received the bad check and make amends, you can spare yourself an extreme amount of hassles.

BAD CHECKS

before calling. When you do call you must ask to speak with a manager or someone with the authority to rectictify this matter. Don't mention anything about the collection agency unless they do first. Mentioning the collection agency right away gives the manager the impression that you are not truly sorry and embarrassed by this incident but more concerned about saving your butt from the debt collectors. So once you have the manager on the phone, besides being very apologetic and embarrassed by this incident escalating to this point, you must convey your sincerity in resolving this problem as fast as possible. Tell the manager that you would be indebted to them and that this will never happen again, if they would just offer you the opportunity to make amends in the form of paying for the check and fees in full TODAY, or at their earliest convenience. Stress to the vendor that you have the cash in your hand at this very moment and that you would be able to deliver it to them today. If this is the first time you have bounced a check with this party they should be receptive to this arrangement. If this is your second time bouncing a check with this same party your chances of success are greatly decreased, but all hope is not lost. If you have bounced a check with this same party more than twice then you should be more concerned with your problem of managing money.

3) <u>Make sure that the collection agency will be notified of this matter being rectified</u>. After you have worked out an agreement and your in the presence of the manager with the cash in hand, very tactfully ask how the course of this matter will be handled in respect to the collection agency being notified that you have cleared this matter up. Act like this is one of your least concerns in making sure that this problem is all taken care of even though it is your main motive for going through all of this trouble. They will usually tell you that the collection agency will be contacted and that you shouldn't hear from them again. Be sure to get some type of **receipt** or letter stating that this matter is all cleared up, this is very important and should not be forgotten. Many times people get very busy and either forget your particular situation or lose records that show that this matter was satisfied. Ask the manager if it would be all right if you would retain their name and phone number as a reference or contact person in case the collection agency needs to speak with someone about this matter. Now the fun part!

4) <u>Contact the collection agency</u>. I know you would love to call the collection agency and harass them as they did you, but please refrain. Even though they would apologize and claim that it was an accident, this little matter could be dragged out, screwed up and sent to the credit bureaus causing you a lot more grief and problems to rectify. They may even note or flag your name in their computer database should you ever be turned over to them again for collections. So it is in your best interest to present them with any copies of your receipts or proof of payment in a courteous manner. If the collection agency has a problem believing you have resolved this matter simply give them the name and phone # of the person who helped you.

5) If you really don't trust the collection agency handling this matter and feel they may place this item on your credit report, follow the instructions in the section on collection agencies and go through the trouble of sending them a **ceasecomm letter**, which will legally prevent them from taking such actions.

"After you have worked out an agreement and you're in the presence of the manager with the cash in hand, very tactfully ask how the course of this matter will be handled in respect to the collection agency being notified that you have cleared this matter up."

Choosing the right steps.

Debt Reduction & Lowering Your Bankcard A.P.R.

OVERVIEW

We will now discuss some of the most common accelerators. When used alone and in combination, accelerators can be used to quickly eliminate your debts. However, not all accelerators are appropriate in all situations. So it is very important to analyze which debt reduction plan would best suit your particular situation in order to effectively reduce your debt.

Debt Compression:

Debt compression is simply the process of obtaining a new loan with a lower interest rate and/or a lower monthly payment and compressing existing loans with higher interests into it. The lower monthly payment creates a margin between the old payment and the new payment. This margin then can be applied towards retiring debts that would most benefit you. As an example, let's suppose you had consumer debts totaling $425 per month, and a financial company determined that a home equity loan could retire the entire amount of the old debt. If the payment on the new home equity loan is $225 per month, an additional $200 would be available to retire the debt. In reality, however, an extremely large percentage of people like you who try a debt compression program on their own have difficulty applying the margin directly to their debt. In almost every case, the margin goes for something else. Even if you did exercise the discipline necessary to put the money into an IRA earning, say 4.5%, you'd be far better off paying off a credit card balance more quickly than scheduled, since you're probably being charged 19% interest or greater.

Employees W-4:

Increasing the number of exemptions on your W-4 form means less money is withheld from your paycheck. If you can increase your number of exemptions, you can create a margin that could be used to pay down debt. This method is very risky for most because you must try and calculate about how much you can increase your exemptions by without owing a wheel barrel of money at the end of the year to Uncle Sam. The other gamble is with your ability to refrain from spending the money and having good self discipline. The extra money each month is like discovering new found wealth. In order to use an accelerator like this you must consult with a tax advisor to discuss your withholding exemptions and have a plan to keep the extra money out of your sight.

Debt Roll Down:

Debt roll down is the process of paying off the shortest-term debt. That payment can then be applied to the next shortest-term debt. This process of rolling down the payments can continue, thereby creating an increasingly larger margin, which can be used to pay debts off in 1/2 to 1/3 the time, saving thousands of dollars in scheduled payments. This accelerator requires

"...not all accelerators are appropriate in all situations. So it is very important to analyze which debt reduction plan would best suit your particular situation to efficiently reduce your debt."

Common Accelerators

very strict financial discipline. Very few people can remain on this type of program for long without professional assistance. A better method, but none the less difficult for discipline, is high interest rate roll down. Same concept as a regular roll down except you began with the credit card or other high interest debt first. It is based on the concept that the exponential growth of the interest due to the higher interest rate is best dealt with first. Again simple math will tell you that your dealt is accumulating faster on those debts with the higher interest so those are the ones that you need to deal with first. A simple example is what should you pay off first, your home mortgage-which is a much larger debt but at a low interest rate of 7.25%, or your credit card which is a smaller amount but has a very much higher interest rate. In theory there is a happy medium, but everybody has a different scenario that they will have to work out. I personally like the high interest roll down. Paying off those high interest cards is like getting rid of a school of loan sharks.

Pulsating Payments:

Pulsating payments is a process to decrease the accumulation of interest on credit card debt. Suppose a credit card company is on a 28-day compounding cycle, with payment due dates on the 30th of the month. Interest due on the 28th will be added to the account balance so you will actually be charged for two extra days each month! At the end of the year, you will have paid interest on 24 extra days, probably without ever knowing it. Interest is accumulated on interest. The result is that a $5,000 credit card debt at 21%, with a minimum payment of 3% of the unpaid balance, will take you about 21 years to pay off! You'll pay $6,732.00 in interest for a total of $11,732.00. Determining the compounding cycle of a credit card company, then making payments at several monthly intervals lowers the principal before the compounding of interest can take place. Just call up each of your cards and ask them all of this pertinent information so you can plan your payments.

Insurance Options:

It is always good sense to shop around for better insurance rates near the expiration dates of your policies. Your home insurance won't make much of a difference with you saving no more than a hundred dollars a year, but you can make a significant cash flow with your automobile policy. This lower premium can create a cash margin that can be applied to debt reduction. You can even play with the higher deductions but always keep some policy in force; it's the law almost everywhere.

Bi-Weekly Payments:

A bi-weekly payment plan is one of the most common accelerators. Bi-weekly payments can cut 8 to 10 years off a 30-year, 8.5% mortgage. This plan divides the monthly mortgage payment into payments being made every two weeks. Twenty-six half payments per year creates a thirteenth payment that goes directly against the principal. There are a lot of companies out there that will try and solicit a whole refinancing program with this concept as a sales point. No magic, just simple arithmetic combined with refinancing your home with its equity. You don't need to pay a company literally thousands of dollars to tell you that.

However, you should be aware that most creditors would not accept bi-weekly payments. Those that do may charge a one-time fee and/or a monthly service charge. To run an amortization schedule, a company might charge as much as $400.

With some mortgage companies a bi-weekly payment plan is not an option. However, if you choose, you can achieve the same result as a bi-weekly payment plan, even though your creditor may not accept bi-weekly payments. If you simply apply a mere $100 toward your principal balance each month, the results are almost identical to the thirteenth payment generated by a bi-weekly payment plan. If you have the capabilities to set up an automatic deposit and deduction with your payroll and mortgage company, you just have that extra $100 deducted each month and applied to the principal. You just consider it gone like your FICA deduction, which is typically three times that amount.

Deferred Interest:
Deferred interest loans, if managed properly, can be a big asset in debt reduction. The idea is that the money that would pay interest is deferred to a later date in the loan amortization. That money becomes available to apply towards debt reduction.
It works like this: Let's suppose you pay $699 monthly on a $100,000 30-year mortgage at a 7.5% fixed rate. Some mortgage lenders can offer you deferred loan rates as low as 4%, which would only require a payment of $450 per month. The $249 margin created by this maneuver can then be applied your debts, which will create a surplus of funds which then can be applied against your mortgage. Through this method, some people can pay $600 or more power-payments per month against their mortgages.

The payments on most deferred interest loans can increase by as much as 7.5% each year. The $450 loan above would increase by $34 ($450.00 x 7.5% = $34.00) the second year, for a total payment of $484. While the margin would be less, keep in mind that during the first year the payment can't increase, and the payments cannot increase more than 7.5% each year. For some people, the rapid acceleration of debt reduction far outweighs the increased annual payments.

ARM

"For those of you who have a Visa or Mastercard with an interest rate of 18% or more, you may be very interested to learn that you may be able to lower your interest rate in about 5 minutes."

Adjustable-Rate Mortgages:

One debt reducing option is to refinance any existing mortgages, consolidating them into one lower payment at a lower interest. A $150,000, 30-year, 8% mortgage could cost 264% of the original mortgage amount. Over sixty percent of the mortgage payment is interest. A lower interest rate greatly reduces the monthly payments, freeing up cash, while also reducing the principal balance.

For instances:

Consider a $150,000.00, 30 year mortgage at 4-5% for an ARM and 8% for a 30-year fixed mortgage. The ARM would cost $800 per month while the 30-year would cost $1,100. The ARM savings of $3,600 annually could be used to pay off debts, reduce mortgage principal or invest. Investing $3,600 at 10% each year for 30 years would build $592,178.00!

Example: If you were to pay off your mortgage in 10 years, and you then invested an $1,100 monthly payment for 20 years at a return of 10%, you'd have $756,016.00! Not to mention the equity in your home!

IMPORTANT: Most people don't realize that interest payments cost $1.00 for every $.15-.30 in tax savings. Tax savings for the interest paid on mortgages does not compensate for what interest costs. Don't be fooled by someone who tries to tell you that it is to owe money on a mortgage because of the tax advantages!

Most ARMs are linked to the Treasury Bill rate. Normally ARM rates cannot increase more than 2% per year to a maximum of six points above the base. If interest rates fall, the ARM rate could decrease accordingly. An ARM works best for clients who have a long-term outlook and may help you become debt free in a very short time.

ARM payments are figured annually on the outstanding mortgage balance. Ideally, clients can lower the outstanding balance quickly so that future payments are figured on the lower balance.

Lowering Your Bankcard A.P.R. In 5 Minutes

For those of you who have a Visa or MasterCard with an interest rate of 18% or more, you may be very interested to learn that you may be able to lower your interest rate in about 5 minutes. '**Balance piracy**' is the term that is used to describe how banks or lending institutions steal customers away from each other by offering consumers a lower interest rate if they transfer their outstanding balances to their bank. Balance piracy offers you the opportunity to lower your interest rate on your credit card balances by either:

Debt Reduction & Lower A.P.R.

1) Transferring your balances on your credit cards to another institution with a lower interest rate.

2) Appearing to your current credit card company that you are seriously contemplating a transfer for a lower interest rate, forcing your bank to offer you a lower interest rate or lose your business.

Everyone should be able to get a better deal on their banks cards **except** for those who 1) have a bankcard that is already paying you back, 2) don't have a balance or 3) have a delinquent payment history (don't pay on time). When I use the term a card that pays you back I am referring to those cards that are affiliated with airlines or car companies. These cards allow you to earn credit with the airlines or car company and are considered to be a bonus in lieu of a lower interest rate. A lower interest rate on these cards is not impossible, but may prove to be more difficult, but never the less worth pursuing. If you do not owe anything on the bankcard you obviously do not need to be concerned with an interest rate because you are not paying any interest. There is a simple procedure to follow to begin lowering your interest rate. All you need is a phone and the cards that you wish to lower the interest rates on. Here are the steps that you need to follow:

1) Get your Visa or MasterCard and locate the 1-800 # for the customer service on back of the card. This is the number that you will need to call. Your bank will have representatives standing by 24 hours a day to help you, but calling between 9-5 p.m. (normal business hours) is preferred. When the operator answers, ask to speak with a credit supervisor. A credit supervisor will not only be more familiar with the 'balance piracy' game but will also have the authority to fulfill your requests. Don't mention the term 'balance piracy.'

2) After you provide the supervisor with the required inf. to access your account, tell them that the reason for your call is you are inquiring about your current interest rate. As soon as they tell you how much it is, sort of sigh and say "oh-kind of high huh." Then proceed and ask them for the pay-off amount on this account. Then tell a little white lie "that you recently received an offer from another bankcard that has a much lower interest rate." Follow up by telling them that you really appreciated the service that they have provided and would love to keep doing business with them, but it is getting very difficult to resist all of these better transfer offers.

The practice of lending institutions to entice you to transfer your balances of your credit cards to their lending institution is called 'Balance piracy'. This practice offers you the opportunity to lower your interest rate on your credit card balances very quickly.

Lowering Your APR

73

You can literally save hundreds if not thousands of dollars in interest payments by lowering your bankcard APR.

3) Lower the hammer! If they have not already offered you a better interest rate, be blunt and ask them if they would be able to match or beat a recent interest rate offer of 7.5%. Unless the bankcard company has some serious problems with their marketing plan they should make you some type of counter offer. It's now up to you to wheel and deal and see how low they will go. If the bankcard company simply refuses to lower your rate then just say "thank you" and hang up.

Look what you can save:

$4,500 balance @ 18% you pay................ $810.00/yr.

$4,500 balance @ 7.5% you pay...............$337.50/yr.

You have just saved **$472.50/yr.** in interest

Rebuilding Your Credit with secured & unsecured credit cards

Hopefully by this time you have reached a point where you are satisfied with the condition of your credit reports and are ready to start rebuilding GOOD credit. There are a few good habits that you are going to have to adopt in order to avoid the mess from which you just got out. First of all, don't go crazy and apply for every type of credit account imaginable. Your credit report may appear to be void of a lot of accounts that you had removed, sending a signal to possible creditors that there may have been a problem in the past. This void is called a **credit gap**. A credit gap may or may not be a bad thing, but it does tip off creditors to inquire deeper into your past, and ultimately resulting in you being turned down for credit. A word of advice is to be very selective in where you apply for credit. The worst thing you want to do at this time is start off your newfound credit with a myriad of **inquiries**.

The best way to overshadow a credit gap or empty credit report is by obtaining a **secured credit card**. Secured credit cards are a good way to establish credit stability and integrity. Here is how secure credit cards work. A bank will offer you a line of credit on a Visa or MasterCard equal to the amount you deposit into a savings account in their bank. The larger the deposit you make, the greater the line of credit. A lot of banks now even offer lines of credit that are 125% or more of your deposit. You will also receive interest on the monies that you deposit into the account. Your deposit basically secures your line of credit, so there is no risk on the part of the bank. Some of the banks will even extend your credit limit beyond the amount of the deposit, refer to out list in the appendix for those banks. Any way you work it, it shows up on your credit report as a **big positive**. After you have shown responsibility with your Visa, at least six months, you should try and obtain credit with Gas companies.

A gas card from familiar names such as Amoco, Texaco or Conoco, is another way to add to your stability. These types of cards are not that difficult to obtain because there isn't a whole lot that you can get carried away with. You should keep good track of both of these types of credit cards, being sure never to miss a payment and staying below the credit limit. Usually, after an ordeal of bad credit, you have a little more knowledge of the consequences you can face and tend to be a little more careful with your spending, hopefully. Your next step should be going to a local furniture store or small outlet and obtaining a <u>small</u> line of credit that you can pay off in a relatively short period of time, like a few months. As with any line of credit, if you show responsible regard for your debts, they will be inclined to extend your line of credit. Just remember, their in business to sell and make money and may not care if you become overextended. So be wary, and don't accept a line of credit, even if they offer, that you may feel is to close to being out of your means.

"A gas card from familiar names such as Amoco, Texaco or Conoco, is another way to add to your stability. The other way is to use out list of banks offering great deals for secured credit card accounts, found in the appendix"

Rebuilding Your Credit.

"The whole name of the game is to build credit worthiness, not merchandise. Eventually you will be back on the road of good credit a little bit wiser than before."

A simple note about the Consumer Credit Counseling Service (CCCS); they are no more than a glorified Collection Agency. They claim to be a non-profit organization, but that is simply a lie! They actually receive 13%-15% of all the money they collect from you. Be realistic, in this particular industry do you believe that there is a company that will manage your money, relieve you from all of your debt without filing a bankruptcy, set up payment plans and counsel you on money management for FREE. Give me a break! Nothing is free in this world and if somebody is trying to pull you into there office with financial fantasies like these, you can bet that there is something that they are not telling you and there is ultimately a scheme behind their efforts. It is all a lie. They put you on payment plans, screw up your credit with bad notations that have their name all over it, and heaven forbid you miss a payment then you are really screwed. It is like working out a deal with the devil, there is always some type of trade off and in this case it is your credit. The creditors pay these people. They receive a percentage of everything they successfully collect---is that non-profit? CCCS may be endorsed by the credit bureaus, but it's because they assist the bureaus in handling the enormous amount of people with credit problems by taking them out of the credit loop. They may provide you with some good information at times. But sometimes, their advice can leave your credit standing in worst shape than when you walked in. Some of their policies, like having you cut up your credit cards, are just too extreme. Let me give you one word of advice, Beware.

The whole name of the game is to build credit worthiness, not merchandise. Eventually you will be back on the road of good credit a little bit wiser than before.

In the appendix you will find a list of financial institutions offering good deals for secured and unsecured credit cards.

SO GOOD LUCK, AND I WISH YOU THE BEST!!!

Special Interest

SAINZ PUBLISHING, LLC

www.legalseries.com

Legal Kits for the Do-It-Yourselfer

Money back satisfaction guarantee

Each book in the series is written so that the average consumer can easily understand the topic without becoming a lawyer. Each book and it's content is scrutinized by our law team for accuracy. You will be transformed into your own personal attorney, able to accomplish tasks with ease while saving literally hundreds if not thousands of dollars by doing it yourself.

Tel: 800-835-2720

Do-It-Yourself Legal Kits

Each Legal Kit doesn't overwhelm you with useless legal jargon. You receive just the facts and the necessary information on the topic in terms you can understand. You also receive step-by-step instructions, legal advice, and all of the forms. You also get a CD-Rom filled with the forms electronically and much more. We make learning and using the law a breeze, in fact we guarantee it! Now you can call mom and let her know that everything has been taken care of by you and the legal experts at Sainz Publishing! .

- Credit Repair Kit
- Bankruptcy Kit
- Wills & Estates Kit
- 101 Legal Contracts Kit
- Estate Planning

Sainz Publishing

SAINZ PUBLISHING, LLC

Sainz Publishing, LLC
P.O. Box 11452
Denver, CO. 80211

Phone: 303-280-4702
Fax: 303-280-5090
Email: info@legalseries.com

Order Form Title

Item #	Description	Qty.	Price	Subtotal

Name

Address

Phone

Method of Payment ☐ Check ☐ Bill Me ☐ Visa ☐ MasterCard ☐ American Express

Credit Card #   Exp. date

Signature

Order total: _____
Tax: _____
Shipping: _____
Total: _____

Earn Income on the Net!

Opportunity

Become a Reseller & Earn $12 Per Order!

You can have your very own Credit Repair Kit Business *FREE OF CHARGE!*

When you become a Reseller, this is what you get for **FREE**!

* Your very own Do-It-Yourself Credit Repair Kit Website
* Professional Ad copy for advertising your website
* Professionally Designed Banners to market your website
* Marketing Support and Strategies
* Home Office Support - Tracking, Shipping, Order Taking

All you have to do is market your website and collect commission checks. No internet experience necessary, If you know how to send email, you can make money!

We collect the payments from your customers, ship the product, handle all customer service, track your sales and cut you monthly commission checks!

There is absolutely nothing for you to purchase!

Jut go to www.FreeInternetOffers.com and sign up! You will receive an email confirmation within 24 hours. You can actually start earning commissions immediately after you receive this email!

www.FreeInternetOffers.com

Frequently Asked Questions

Frequently Asked Questions

A Bankruptcy should always be the very last thing you should consider.

This section is made up of actual credit questions asked on our web site.

Q. OK you say you can fix bad credit. Can you do anything about unpaid credit card debt, medical bills. I am unable to pay the amount of debt I have occurred. Will your program help me or do I need to file bankruptcy before you can help.

A. A Bankruptcy should always be the very last thing you should consider. Our book can help. There is a whole section dedicated to debt reduction that details 8 different methods that one can use to reduce debt before doing anything as drastic and detrimental as a BK. First of all never run from your problems. You need to contact every creditor that you have and talk to them. Explain your circumstances and they all have plans that they can put you on to help you out without destroying your credit. For instances, a credit card company can suspend all charging privileges on your account, without totally closing it, and put you on a payment plan that will drastically reduce your payments almost by 50%. It is more advantageous for the medical billing companies and other creditors to work with you on payments to ascertain all of the owed debt than to sell off your account to a collection company for a smaller percentage of the amount owed. This is not always the case, because some companies would rather sell off your account than deal with all of the hassles of billing, but our book can help you deal with those types of companies as well. Our book can definitely help you if you want to help yourself. Avoid a BK if at all possible.

Q. I would like to know if this is also for Wisconsin? This does sound to good to be true, and how come nobody else knows about it? could this be a scam or should I ask some lawyers about this? I've had some late payments on a bill and that is what is bringing my credit down. They say bad credit history stays on your report for 7 years, is this true.

A. The Credit Repair Kit is applicable for all 52 states in the United States including Guam & Puerto Rico. The Kit has been sent and used effectively by many of our Armed Forces Personnel as far as Japan, China and Germany. The truth is the book has been offered on TV and has helped literally tens of thousands of consumers with their credit dilemmas. The book has been offered nationwide for the past five years. Thanks to the internet we are now getting a great deal more of exposure and recognition as the nations leading resource for All credit matters. Everything in the book is based of facts, the law, and actual true experiences. It is 100% legal and parts of the book have actually been contributed by some of the lawyers of the two law firms that we are affiliated with. We are not a company that is trying to scam anybody, but rather a company that has found a way to help the consumer by providing legal and effective ways to use the credit laws that were

Credit Card Debt

93

You can challenge almost everything on your credit reports even bankruptcy items and total bankruptcies, legally.

established by the Federal Trade Commission to the consumers best advantage. Negative marks on your credit report will remain there for 7 years from the date of last activity, and possibly longer, unless you do something about it. I encourage you to use the laws and the dispute process to remove information on your credit report that you believe may be misleading, questionable, outdated, incorrect, or you believe to be in any way misreported. I am sure you can find something wrong with a large percentage of the items on all three of your credit reports. There is almost 99% of the time something questionable about your credit reports. If Senators, NFL football players, and millionaires use this book effectively, so can you. Yes, this kit can help you to avid waiting 7 dreadful years.

Q. Your kit sounds great but I am in my 2nd year of a Chap. 13 and there's nothing short of having my credit file completely erased! But what I like to (I heard it from some of my friends is that I can get another Social security card! Is this possible? Is this Legal? and if it is how can I get info on this!

A. First of all getting a second social security number is totally illegal and we highly recommend that you don't involve yourself with anything of that nature, it is not worth it. A lot of the individuals selling or claiming they have information of this type are usually just ripping off desperate consumers. Those that are actually doing this will go to Federal prison when caught. We don't promote nor do we condone any such process. On the other hand, our Kit has been successfully used to remove even bankruptcies. You may ask how is this possible and how can it be legal. It is totally legal and performed everyday. How it is done is using the credit laws to your advantage. You have the legal right to intervene into the processes of the credit bureau at any time to make sure that the personal information that they are selling about you is absolutely 100% correct. You can challenge almost everything on your credit reports even bankruptcy items and total bankruptcies, legally. It is very common for human error to be a factor in a great deal of the items on your credit report. It is your job as a weary consumer to be scrutinizing every part of every item for any possible errors and believed errors. Once you find one or believe you have found one, it is your right within the law to dispute that item and MAKE the credit bureau prove that this item is reported exactly as it states. If for whatever reason, in the case of public record items such as a bankruptcy, they cannot verify the information as being 100% accurate they have to remove the item per your request. A frequent scenario is they are understaffed to handle such requests.

Maybe the information has been archived and their computer records backed up and it requires to much time for them to restore those records, whatever, if they cannot get back to the credit bureaus within 30+ days, it must come off if you request it. Just as if you go into a courtroom to fight a speeding ticket and the officer does not show up, the ticket is dismissed and all charges dropped. Why, because you are innocent until proven guilty, make them prove it or make them remove it. This is the beauty of living in America; you might as well use your freedoms to your advantage or just sit back and suffer the consequences, but don't complain because you are the one who chooses to do nothing about it!

Q. I was very happy to see your web site. My credit is not perfect, so I am somewhat limited to what I can and can't do as far as purchasing power is concerned. However, I would like to purchase your kit, but I need to know a little more about it. What actually comes in the kit and how will it help me.

A. "As Seen on TV". This book cuts straight to the chase and shows you how to get results! It is like no other book on the market because of it's true to life examples and audacity to let the cat out of the bag. Almost every other book on the market simply preaches the law because they are afraid of criticism. This book holds nothing back and shows you how to test the limits of the law. We don't preach, just teach! This laminated soft cover book is comprised of 11 chapters of experience, instructing consumers with Step-by-Step Examples and Samples on how to legally and effectively rectify credit dilemmas from all three of their credit reports. It also teaches consumers (8) different techniques for reducing debt and rebuilding credit, how to STOP debt collectors with a single letter, reduce bankcard A.P.R. in (5) minutes, and every legal credit cleaning technique the credit bureaus wish you did not know. Its 100% legal, totally within the realms of the law and referred by several law firms and used by mortgage companies across the nation, because of its effectiveness to quickly get results for its users. Guaranteed satisfaction or your money back.

A wave of change is sweeping the nation in how credit matters are handled by the credit bureaus, and Sainz Enterprises, LLC with their mastery of handling credit matters easily and effectively, is riding the crest. After many years of writing, researching, and actually testing different methods and techniques, Joe was able to compile a very functional and totally legal method for resolving credit dilemmas. He has discovered that one can easily use the very same laws that are hindering ones credit, to actually help an individual.

"As Seen on TV". This book cuts straight to the chase and shows you how to get results!

Money-Back Guarantee

An Educational Do-It-Yourself
CREDIT REPAIR KIT

The FREE CD enclosed has all of the necessary Forms from within the book in a reproducible form of Microsoft Word.

Many are still under the impression that if something is placed on their credit that it is forged in time for a period of 7 to 10 years. Well it is, and in some instances for longer periods of time, unless you do something about it, But how!! Our nation is built on a system of checks and balances and the premise that you are innocent until proven guilty. The credit bureaus are non-government-affiliated companies selling your personal information for a profit, make them earn their money. Laws such as the Fair Credit Reporting Act, written by the FTC, states that the individual has the right to intervene into the practices of the credit bureaus to make sure that the information that is being distributed is absolutely 100% accurate or not distributed! Make them do their jobs of verifying the information. Sainz Enterprises, LLC with their Do-It-Yourself CREDIT REPAIR KIT will teach you how to do it effectively AND LEGALLY.

A FREE CD-Rom accompanies each book. The CD contains all of the necessary Forms from within the book in a reproducible form of Microsoft Word. This makes it easy to quickly get started and produce all necessary letters to begin clearing up your credit within 20 minutes. You can then help your family and friends very easily. You will also receive 100 FREE fun and useful licensed computer programs (utilities, games, productivity, etc..), Internet promotions -including Unlimited Internet Access and Important credit links, and all this with a 100% money back satisfaction guarantee.

Q. My mother always taught me that if its to good to be true than it probably isn't true... My husband and I had to file bankruptcy 2yrs ago. He had been ill for 2 months and lost a lot of time from work..(with 5 children to feed, disability doesn't quite cut it) Since then its been difficult, to say the least. Sometimes I feel as though we have been fed to the bottom feeders who take advantage of people, who don't have many options. Credit card companies who charge an arm and a leg just to have a card with extremely high interest..(these offers come in regularly) Get this, advertisements on the radio who say yes, even if you went bankrupt you can still buy a car from us NOT!! That's only if you can still afford the car with unreasonably high interest tacked on it..My point is that I am very skeptical, now that I have experience with companies who prey on people with bad credit. If you are different and sincere in that your (kit) can and will help without taking advantage of the unfortunate. Could you please send a little more information on how this is possible. How can you help remove or repair our credit with a bankruptcy on it legally?

The most effective methods for resolving credit issues have been outlines and samples given with easy step-by-step instructions.

A. I am sorry for your recent unfortunate circumstances. I hate to hear about situations such as yours, but I can definitely relate. The author has been through a great deal of credit dilemmas, in fact that is how the whole concept and idea for the book was derived. The Credit Repair Kit book was written by a consumer for the consumer after dealing with all of the tribulations, runaround, and hassles of trying to resolve credit issues with the credit bureaus. It is becoming a little easier to deal with the bureaus this past year but when the author begin dealing with credit issues 11 years ago, you had to rely on all of your abilities of research, phone calls, cunning, creativeness, and a whole lot of persistence. What came out of all of credit problems was a seasoned veteran who was constantly bombarded by friends and family with credit questions. After 6 years of helping others with every imaginable credit dilemma, the new expert on credit, decided to take the advise of a lot of people and venture to help people with their credit professionally. After five more years of documenting what works and what doesn't and consulting with two separate law firms on a regular basis, you have a second edition Educational Do-It-Yourself credit Repair Kit that is based on true to life experiences. The most effective methods for resolving credit issues have been outlines and samples given with easy step-by-step instructions. These methods have been taught for 11 years to tens of thousands of consumers nationwide, including crewmen aboard a ship sailing around the southern tip of Africa and all the way to China and Germany. We don't believe in ripping off consumers, only helping them. When the author was down and out he was in desperate for help but there was none to be found, he had to figure it out for himself. You cannot go wrong with a product that has such a low price tag and a 30 day money back guarantee. As far as family the author now has 3 daughters and a son and is a firm believer in family and faith. There are a lot of rip-off artists out there and you should be steer clear of any credit clinics that make you a lot of unbelievable promises, especially if they want a lot of money up front or fees such as $100item or $1000.00 to clean your credit. You will wonder how you ever did without this credit treasure.

Step-By-Step Credit Repair

So If things don't work out and you get a divorce and in court it is decided that one of the two parties will be responsible for making payments on certain financial obligations, the creditor doesn't care.

Q. I have been divorced for ten years. I have maintained excellent credit but my x has not. our divorce gave him some property that was in both our names and my decree says that he is responsible for the payments. un fortunately, the loans remained in both our names and he has been in a foreclosure and it shows up on my credit. when I apply for loans, I have been turned down because of his bad payment history. Can I get this turned around on my credit?

A. You have a very common problem that is shared by a lot of divorced couples. The law states that a divorce decree does not supercede credit contractual obligations entered into by both parties while being married. In other words, if you get a joint account such as a visa or buy a home together while married you both are responsible for that debt, even after getting a divorce. So If things don't work out and you get a divorce and in court it is decided that one of the two parties will be responsible for making payments on certain financial obligations, the creditor doesn't care. All the creditor cares about is timely payments and it doesn't matter who makes them as long as there made. In the creditor's eyes a divorce decree doesn't matter and as far as the law is concerned the creditor is right. So, here is how you deal with this. If you must go through a divorce and one party is obligated for certain bills, you must immediately contact that creditor and make them aware of the circumstances. Close all accounts that are joint so that no further expenditures can be incurred. Depending on the balance of the account it can be an easy or troublesome ordeal. If your balance is $0 you can close the account and that is it. If there is a balance the creditor holds whoever opened it responsible, they don't care if the court says one or the other has to pay from here on out, they just want to be paid. We have had clients successfully send in court documents with letters expressing the circumstances and stating they are no longer responsible for further charges and they wish to be removed from the account. The creditors, Novvus and Visa, agreed to clear them from the account once they sent in 50% of the current balance, they were then relinquished of all responsibility and credit status maintained. In your case a letter from the attorney and perhaps the judge, we have clients successfully obtain letters, and send it to the mortgage company requesting that the client be relieved of responsibility and asking that the negative items associated with this client's credit reports be removed. But, let it be understood that you are relinquishing ownership of this property as well, as you may already done. I guess you can't have it all.

If it has to do with your credit it is covered in this book!

Q. Hi. I just wanted to run two things by you. One, how is this different from the AOL CreditAlert, and similar products? They provide you with a copy (of a translation) of your report from the 3 main agencies, and then these blank forms to send in disputes (but they are basically just letterhead). Also, I wanted to let you know that you have a typo on your site!   ...credit that you deserve. But don't just take my word for it... what have you got to loose? Just Order the Kit and Check it out... I am sure that you meant to type 'lose' not 'loose', so I thought I would point that out! :)

A. I am uncertain of AOL's CreditAlert and therefore I am uncertain.But, if CreditAlert is anything like Privacy Guard or some service that alerts consumers to possible problems with their credit reports or provides the consumers with periodic credit reports, we are nothing like that. We provide the consumer with the tools and information to resolve any type of credit problems themselves. Our information is contained in a very comprehensive 11 chapter book that contains everything you need to know about how the entire credit system works. How to obtain and translate all three of your credit reports. It also details every possible thing that can appear on each credit report, and how you go about resolving any type of problem with any of these items. It also has a chapter on dealing with debt collectors, resolving bad checks, rebuilding your credit after resolving all of your credit issues, as well as an entire section on (8) different types of debt reduction plans. The 160 page book also contains a chapter on secured credit cards and provides you with a list of over 30 financial institutions with all of their card offers and toll-free numbers. Not only does the book provide the consumer with all of this invaluable information based on years of experience from a credit restoration expert, but it also provides the consumer with step-by-step instructions on how to do everything it teaches. The book also goes as far as proving you with actual proven effective examples and samples for resolving typical issues, but then it provides you with every form you will ever need, already drafted with example disputes. If it has to do with your credit it is covered in this book. To make it even better the book also comes with a ton of FREE software on CD-Rom the whole family can appreciate as well as with all of the afore mentioned forms electronically in Microsoft Word.

Q. Hi, Thank you very much for speaking with me on the telephone. I have a couple of questions regarding your information, but first a synopsis of my situation:

My financial picture at present is very bleak. I have about 8 credit cards which have all been charged off or sold to third parties for collection. My unsecured credit card debt is currently about $35,000 and climbing (the interest, you see, tends to rack up very quickly). I am facing the possibility of a Chapter 7 or 13 bankruptcy. Several months ago, I lost my job,so I am

Examples that are proven success stories

currently unemployed. My credit history is so badly damaged that I was told a bankruptcy can't hurt me any further, despite collections agencies' cries of "Don't do it, don't do it!". I don't have enough credit to buy a hot dog, at this point. I know I have a LOT of 30-, 60-, 90- day delinquencies on my credit history, and even higher (some as high as 120 days or more). I can only be approved for a secured credit card, where I have to send money. Is the claim on your advertising true, that items like these can be eliminated from my credit history? How? They usually stay on there for a while until you build up your credit again... And what about a bankruptcy? Rumor has it that it stays on there for 7 - 10 years. Can THAT be wiped out? And are all my rights of having this negative information removed from my files clearly spelled out in the Fair Credit Act? Where can I view a copy of this Act?

These are some of the questions I have regarding your information. At this point, I will have quite a bit of difficulty scraping up the $39.95 needed to get your book. I currently do NOT have a credit card, but I may still be able to use my debit card from my bank. However, even THAT has been frozen. The only saving grace here is through my checking account.

Most of the time the credit grantor will agree to settle for the plan and chances are they will settle for a smaller amount than you actually owed.

A. I hate to turn away business, but I would rather be honest with you and tell you to save the $40 cost of our program and use it to get back on your feet with a job search. To be quite honest with you, your problems are quite extensive and even though our book is an excellent resource for resolving all of your credit issues, your first priority should not be purchasing from us but obtaining a job. Your success with our product is going to be dependent on you having some financial resources in the terms of some monies to negotiate with creditors. A job and our product together can solve your problems, and I will now tell you how and answer your questions so that when you get a little more established we can work together to solve your problems. Paul, it may seem impossible, but try to avoid a bankruptcy. Call each of the credit card companies that have charged off your account and tell them that you are currently unemployed, but that you have access to some funds that you had saved up. Ask them if they would be willing to make a deal where you would agree to make some small payments. Most of the time the credit grantor will agree to settle for the plan and chances are they will settle for a smaller amount than you actually owed. They will do this with the belief that a smaller amount of money is better than no money at all. Never ever deal with the collection agencies! By Law you do not have to deal with them unless they decide to take you to court on a judgement. If the collection agencies are bugging you, immediately send them a cease communication letter; this will stop them from ever harassing you again. You are offered this legal letter with our product, in the book and electronically on a CD-Rom (MS-Word). Our book also teaches you how to negotiate a deal with the creditors and provides the forms for this as well. You can also deal with all of the late payments as well with the dispute process and some diligence; this is covered in detail within a chapter in the book. I have helped consumers remove items as simple as late payments to as serious as entire bankruptcies and judgements. You use the law to do this, and it is proven successful. It is like going into court and pleading innocent and making them prove you guilty. If there is a simple technicality the entire case will be thrown out, the same with items on your credit report. If they cannot prove it they can't distribute it, thus remove it from the credit report. You can receive a copy of the fair credit-reporting act by calling your local Federal Trade Commission and they will send you a FREE copy.

Uncle Sam can be easy to work with and can be accommodating if you call up the IRS and work a deal out.

Q. I saw your information and was wondering if it works with tax liens. There was no mention of them.

A. Yes, but Uncle Sam can come after in a lot of different ways. You may be able to get the tax lien from being reflected on your credit report, but it does not relieve you from the obligation. I have helped people remove these public record items but at the same time I have seen the government go after these people in numerous ways such as intercepting their tax returns, garnishing wages, and seizing property and entire bank accounts. Uncle Sam can be easy to work with and can be accommodating if you call up the IRS and work a deal out. Try to limit the information that you give them and be as nice as you can tolerate. Again, you can remove the items by the dispute process. You gamble, within all rights of the law, on the fact that the public records office, who has your information housed, will not respond in the allotted time to the credit bureau and be forced to remove the item by time default. This is done everyday within the realm of the law, but it is pretty hard to stop Uncle Sam.

The whole turn around process can take up to 6 weeks. It may be a little faster depending on the speed of the credit bureau and the time of the year for the U.S. mail.

Q. Hello, I would like to know more about how this works. Could you please send me more information via email. Also I would like to know do I still need to pay my bills (credit cards) or should I consolidate and pay one monthly note. Do you all deal with bill consolidation and how will I know if that is a good option.

A. Although our book DOES offer (8) different debt consolidation plans the main focus of our book is to offer the consumer a wealth of information on dealing with derogatory credit on their credit reports. The book is based on 12 years of experience by a credit restoration expert on dealing with bad credit issues. The book incorporates experience with existing law, and is associated with two law firms that have contributed to the accuracy of the book. When dealing with debt, if you have the resources it will be better for you to try and consolidate your bills, especially if you can secure a loan based on an owned property such as your home (second mortgage). You must still pay all of your creditors until the said time that the loan is secured and payment in full to the creditors has been received.

Q. How long after you have mailed the forms in will it be until your credit is perfect? Even if you have had to file bankruptcy in the last year?

A. If your NOT dealing with a bankruptcy, it takes a week to have the US mail deliver the letter and get it into processing by the credit bureaus. They then have 30 days to verify the information as being accurate or remove it. They then send you out a new credit report that reflects the corrected information on your new report. This may take another week. The whole turn around process can take up to 6 weeks. It may be a little faster depending on the speed of the credit bureau and the time of the year for the US mail. When dealing with a bankruptcy there is a lot more to do, and it has to be broken into several disputes, a good time frame is a year. You cannot just dispute everything on your credit report because they will send it back to you stamped "Frivolous & Irrelevant". This means that they do not believe you and take it as a joke. You must break it down over several months, disputing pieces of it first. You may have items that appear on your credit report more than once these must go first. You then wait a month and dispute the original main items and eventually the entire bankruptcy. Your credit problems weren't created over night and they won't be resolved overnight, but they can be resolved! We don't publish or promote any fraudulent acts, in fact everything we teach is within the realm of the law. Our book is recommended by attorneys so it has to be. We know how to use the law to get results.

Q. Hi, my name is George. I am much interested in your kit, but my question to you is the following: your money back guarantee is for 30 days; how much time would be needed until the changes would positively be noticed on my credit report?

A. If your NOT dealing with a bankruptcy, it takes a week to have the US mail deliver the letter and get it into processing by the credit bureaus. They then have 30 days to verify the information as being accurate or remove it. They then send you out a new credit report that reflects the corrected information on your new report. This may take another week. The whole turn around process can take up to 6 weeks. It may be a little faster depending on the speed of the credit bureau and the time of the year for the US mail. Your probably in question about the guarantee being 30 days and the first results 5-6 weeks. The answer to this is very simple. When you receive the book, please take the time to read through it. The information that is contained within will not only enlighten you but it may shock you. There is a lot that the average consumer does not know when it comes to credit and their actual rights. The information and knowledge gained is by far worth a lot more than just $40. We don't believe in ripping the consumer off only educating them. We are looking to become the nations best resource for credit restoration information and if we are offering bad information or charging outrageous prices we will never achieve our goals. We truly believe that once you open up the book and try out some of the software, that we include for free, you will agree that this offer is to good to be true. You will hesitate even lending the book to friends, let alone sending it back to us. We give you thirty days when most of the competition will not even consider this because of their quality. We believe in our product and so will you!

Q. In my case, I have 6 credit cards; one of them raised the interest rates to beyond realistic norms (27 %). I am looking for 1 or 2 credit cards with low interest rates to close all the others. But I am in a fix. No credit card company would offer me an unsecured high credit facility because of my current credit cards.
P.S I have a good credit history.
Would your kit help me?

A. The reason you are having difficulty is the cards you are currently carrying probably have very high balances. When creditors look at this they see the balances are not dropping and you become more of a risk. If you wanted you could just dump all of the cards in a bankruptcy, even though that would be idiotic.

When you receive the book, please take the time to read through it. The information that is contained within will not only enlighten you but it may shock you.

Reduce your high balances

As far as our product goes we provide the consumer with the tools and information to resolve any type of credit problems themselves.

But this is what the financial institutions see. What you need to do is try and get a loan and try and pay off some of the cards. One way of reducing some of the debt is to actually close some of the cards to charging, but not entirely closes them. This will reduce the payment on each. You then apply the remaining monies that you were normally paying to the minimal balances on each card and focus them on the highest balance card that you have, until it is paid off. For instance you have two cards that you were normally paying $75.00month on and have the payments reduced to $40.00. You take the remaining $35.00 and apply it to the second card monthly payment. But if your talking (6) cards, the extra amounts applied to the single card that you are focusing on paying off, will be substantial; 6 cards x $35.00 = $210.00 + normal payment. Although our book DOES offer (8) different debt consolidation plans the main focus of our book is to offer the consumer a wealth of information on dealing with derogatory credit on their credit reports. A credit restoration expert on dealing with bad credit issues bases the book on 12 years of experience. The book incorporates experience with existing law, and is associated with two law firms that have contributed to the accuracy of the book. When dealing with debt, if you have the resources it will be better for you to try and consolidate your bills, especially if you can secure a loan based on an owned property such as your home (second mortgage). Our book is filled with tips such as these and I am sure you will find it to benefit you tremendously.

Q. Please tell me what all is included in this kit. What about company charge off, is that included also?

A. Dear Jan, we specifically deal with charge offs in one of our main sections of the book. As far as our product goes we provide the consumer with the tools and information to resolve any type of credit problems themselves. Our information is contained in a very comprehensive 13 chapter book that contains everything you need to know about how the entire credit system works. How to obtain and translate all three of your credit reports. It also details every possible thing that can appear on each credit report, and how you go about resolving any type of problem with any of these items. . It also has a chapter on dealing with debt collectors, resolving bad checks, rebuilding your credit after resolving all of your credit issues, as well as an entire section on (8) different types of debt reduction plans. The 160 page book also contains a chapter on secured credit cards and provides you with a list of over 30 financial institutions with all of their card offers and toll-free numbers.

SECTION TWELVE

Not only does the book provide the consumer with all of this invaluable information based on years of experience from a credit restoration expert, but it also provides the consumer with step-by-step instructions on how to do everything it teaches. The book also goes as far as proving you with actual proven effective examples and samples for resolving typical issues, but then it provides you with every form you will ever need, already drafted with example disputes. If it has to do with your credit it is covered in this book. To make it even better the book also comes with a ton of FREE software on CD-Rom the whole family can appreciate as well as with all of the afore mentioned forms electronically in Microsoft Word.

Q. How can this work for me? Not only do I have bad credit, I owe everyone and their brother money. Sears, Student Loan, Columbia, gas, etc., etc. Thousands of dollars that I had accumulated over 3 years ago. I now have a pretty good job $35-$40 thousand a year, but I have no idea how to even start paying these bills back. I thought about going to credit counseling, but I don't want to get locked into something. I owe $800 for my student loan, which they will take from my tax return this year. My goal is to build a house. I have the land and the ability to pay a house payment, but my credit sucks so bad that I feel like it will never happen. I am tired of paying what could be a house payment for my rent. I was given credit cards with a minimum wage, part-time job as soon as I had enrolled in college. I thought it was the greatest thing in the world. I am 29 years old now, and I realize that these companies are just taking advantage of all of these college students. I also realize that I need to purchase a new home soon so that it is paid for by the time I retire.

A. Dear Craig, this kit it almost a perfect product for you! The reason I say this is your situation resembles the situation that I was in when I began repairing credit, my own. I agree, with you about the credit card situation and college. The very same thing happened to me while in college and turned into a career for me. One of the first things you need to do is take care of the student loan. This is a very quick fix and can actually help your credit within 6 months. You can actually make payment s for 6 months and it will be removed from the default status and reported on your credit reports as if you had never missed a payment, perfect status.This is an incentive from Uncle Sam to encourage defaultedstudent loan holders to take care of their obligations.

One of the first things you need to do is take care of the student loan. This is a very quick fix and can actually help your credit within 6 months.

Students are likely targets

If you have the money and your accounts are 3 or more years delinquent, you have an excellent chance for some very quick and most impressive results.

Second, before you may anything, don't. You need to evaluate each and every item to make sure that you will not damage your credit even further by assuming the best thing to do is pay everything off. Our book teaches you what to pay and what not to pay and why. In most circumstances you can actually be worse off by paying off a creditor. There is something referred to as the 7-year cycle. This is the amount of time that a charged off or delinquent account can stay on your credit report without any monetary activity. By just sending in a payment or signing an agreement to pay, you automatically restart the 7-year period from the date that they receive the monies or signed document from you. You in particular need to get your money together and start playing "lets make a deal" with each and every creditor that you have that is derogatory, but first you need to play the dispute game first. After all disputing has cleaned up its portion of derogatory items you then start negotiating. By doing this you can negotiate all of the negative items off of your credit report, how is this you may ask? You have what they want and they have what you want. Creditors or collection agencies want money and you want a signed letter vowing to remove the negative items from your credit report. This is how it is done, and believe me it works, cash-money is a very powerful bargaining tool! If you have the money and your accounts are 3 or more years delinquent, you have an excellent chance for some very quick and most impressive results. I love your type of problems because my Kit is designed based on your exact scenario and you make me look really good. You need to really go out on a limb (sarcasm) and gamble $40.00 on a worth while opportunity to change your entire life!

Q. My credit is bad, and I still owe about $30K that I don't want to pay, but cant claim bankruptcy again. Its been about 4 years since any new debt has been added to my credit. Does your program cover people in my situation.

A. Your entire situation is covered with this thorough book of credit. Be very careful in your unwillingness to pay back the $30K. On the other hand you can't squeeze blood from a turnip. What ever the reasons are you need to either become proficient at disputing items on your credit report which will result in many of the items being forced off of your credit reports. You will most definitely be left with a few stubborn items that disputing just can't get rid of. These stubborn items need to be taken care of by negotiations with the collection agency or original creditor. You need to be able to produce some money as a bargaining block with these stubborn accounts.

Either way our book details every single scenario and the best way to deal with it. Our 11 chapters and 160 pages of experience will give you examples, samples, and step-by-step instructions on how to perform everything. We also give you the forms already filled out with samples so even your child can help you with your disputing homework.

Either way our book details every single scenario and the best way to deal with it.

Q. Many financial types say there is no such thing as repair services that really work. Please tell me how you can repair, and I will buy the package.

A. There is no such thing as a quick fix, guaranteed, super clean overnight credit cleaning process. We use the term 'credit repair' more as a descriptive term that consumers can relate to. Your credit problems more than likely didn't occur overnight and they won't disappear overnight either. Even using the laws to clear off inaccurate information off of your credit report takes time. There is probably something on one of your reports that does not belong there and we can teach you to recognize and correct the problem, or in other words repair it. In fact, almost all credit reports contain some kind of errors. These errors may be attributed to mis-reporting on the part of the creditor, credit bureau, or in most situations, human error. You have probably heard the term that is used a lot in reference to computers, "garbage in, garbage out." Simply putting it, a simple misspelling or typo error can go a long way when in comes to credit reporting. It is not the computer's fault, it is the person who is operating the computer who is to blame. Needless to say, there is probably some outdated, misreported, mistaken identity, spelling or date error, somewhere on your credit report. We can help you find all of the errors a lot of people overlook and teach you the most efficient way for resolving your dilemma. It is like taking your car for a tune up and telling them to make it run as best as possible. This is what we consider repair. If they dropped a whole new engine in your car, that would be a different story.

We are NOT selling techniques on how to obtain new credit files or anything illegal. We are teaching you how to use the credit laws to your best advantage. If somebody is distributing private information on you, it had better be 100% accurate or they're in big trouble. It is totally within your rights of the law to make sure that any information that is being sold about you is verifiably 100% correct. You therefore have the right to intervene into the processes of the credit bureaus and make them prove the validity of the information that they are selling about you, it is only fair. Our whole government is based on a checks and balances system. The president of the US has to follow this rule and the credit bureaus as well. Now, if they can't verify something as being 100% correct how is it legal for them to distribute that information? It's not, they have to stop distributing it and remove it from your file.

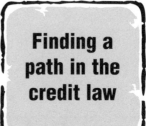

Finding a path in the credit law

Everything we teach in the book is totally legal and within the all realms of the law. When anybody goes to court they take a lawyer with them, why? Because they know the law and how to use the law to receive the most favorable outcome. Do you know the credit laws and what can and cannot be done within the full extent of the laws? We can help!

Q. We don't have $40.00 to just give to someone just because they claim it "really" works. With so many scams on the net these days, it's really sounds too good to be true. Due to a severe knee injury, my husband was placed on total disability by social security at a very young age, that only leaves me to work. Of course he gets his MONTHLY check, and I my measly paychecks every two weeks, but it's never enough to get caught up. We would like very much to get these past debts off our backs but have not found any means short of bankruptcy. If this is a real deal AWESOME!!!!!!!! But, I hope you can understand my doubts. With the little income we have, it's hard to turn loose of so much money on a chance.

A. We love to help out people such as yourself, especially when you have a true need for assistance. If you decide to order the Kit, please write back to the address given within your package and the actual author will give you a phone number that you can contact to discuss a refund and free credit assistance. We truly believe in faith, helping one another, and a great deal of Karma---what comes around goes around! Our experience in dealing with circumstances such as yours, will most definitely be of great service to you. We can most definitely help you with reducing your debt with one of the (8) methods that we teach, thus freeing up some money to negotiate some deals with your creditors to clear up some of the derogatory information on your credit reports. Order the book and we will help your to help yourself. Please don't file a bankruptcy without trying our product first, it will be well worth every minute of your time and monetary investment. You nothing to lose and everything to gain!

Q. Hi, I was just reading about your kit and want to ask a few questions if you don't mind. First of all, my husband and I filed bankruptcy a year ago & I was wondering how we can clear up our credit after doing that? We can't do anything on credit. We have a teenager that needs a car, but we can't get one. My next question is how long does it take to clear up your credit? And can you pay by check for your kit? I don't want to order it on-line. Thank you for your time. Hope to hear from you soon!

A. You can send in a check or money order for your purchase, but I can assure you that all of our transactions on-line are safe. If your NOT dealing with a bankruptcy, it takes a week to have the US mail deliver the letter and get it into processing by the credit bureaus. They then have 30 days to verify the information as being accurate or remove it. They then send you out a new credit report that reflects the corrected information on your new report. This may take another week. The whole turn around process can take up to 6 weeks. It may be a little faster depending on the speed of the credit bureau and the time of the year for the US mail. When dealing with a bankruptcy there is a lot more to do, and it has to be broken into several disputes, a good time frame is a year. You cannot just dispute everything on your credit report because they will send it back to you stamped "Frivolous & Irrelevant". This means that they do not believe you and take it as a joke. You must break it down over several months, disputing pieces of it first. You may have items that appear on your credit report more than once these must go first. You then wait a month and dispute the original main items and eventually the entire bankruptcy. Your credit problems weren't created over night and they won't be resolved overnight, but they can be resolved! We don't publish or promote any fraudulent acts, in fact everything we teach is within the realm of the law. Our book is recommended by attorneys so it has to be. We know how to use the law to get results. You need to begin work on your credit immediately so that you can help your kids out with a Car!

Q. I am very interested in this, as I filed bankruptcy 2 years ago, and cannot get a bank loan at all. What does this do, when a local bank had a loan that was written off, don't all the banks have that record as now? And if so, how can that be taken care of, that will still be on record. You say it is a money back guarantee, how does one know if that is really true?

A. What happens when you go to the bank and apply for a loan is the bank has accounts with at least two of the credit bureaus if not all three of them. They take your information, social security number, birth date, name and address and contact the credit bureaus for the most recent credit information that is being distributed about you. At this point they will evaluate your credit based on a point system that results with a credit score. Based on this score they will decline or approve you for a loan. There are other factors that may also weigh in to their decision. Factors that may affect their decision are how long you have banked with them, the extent of derogatory information on your credit, and a big factor will be if you have collateral. They will then take all this into account and either approve or decline you. The minute they pull your credit report it is documented on your credit report as an Inquiry for the period of two years.

The minute they pull your credit report it is documented on your credit report as an Inquiry for the period of two years.

Our book can help you resolve all of your problems with a 30 day money back guarantee and you can walk into the bank with some confidence that your chances of approval just have dramatically approved.

The bank may keep their records of this attempt for probably no more than 6 months. This is not to say that you couldn't walk into the bank two weeks later and you told them that everything was all cleared up and they would try it again. They may look at you a little funny and may not even believe you, but I am sure they would attempt it, this is how they make money. Our book can help you resolve all of your problems with a 30 day money back guarantee and you can walk into the bank with some confidence that your chances of approval just have dramatically approved. You can either wait 10 years or you can take control and get legal results...NOW!

Q. I seen your website today on the internet and have a couple questions as I am not sure even your kit can help me and/or my husband on this. My husbands bad credit consist of his ex-wife using his social security number. When he applies for credit her name appears not his. He has talked with credit bureaus as well as social security office and they tell him he has to write to every person on the report and tell them the bill is not his. Well, that would take years to do as his credit report is now about 10 pages long. So will your kit help there? As for me, I had a student loan out that I simply forgot about as the school ended up being fraud and supposedly the student loans were cancelled. Well, the loan was purchased to three different companies over the 12 years and they just now found me and are asking for 3 times the amount of the loan. I heard this was past the stipulated time period and even as a student loan should not be on my credit report nor me having to deal with it. At this time, they have a garnishment on my husband's tax refund as I am not employed. Here in Idaho they can only keep half of it. But still this is not my husband's obligation and after not contacting me until 12 years later I do not believe it should be mine. We are presently preparing to buy a home and do not want this situation in a mess for us. So any advice you can give and if the kit will wipe these out please let me know via email.

A. Dear Glenda,

I love to hear from persons as yourself or at least with credit situations such as yours. Our Credit repair Kit is designed especially for consumers who have this type of problem simply because it is one of the most commonly occurring credit issues. Divorce is always as very difficult ordeal and it is a real shame when a person has to deal with credit matters on top of it all. I am certain we can help you. As far as your first problem with the social security number being associated or on the credit report. It is the responsibility of the credit bureau to do all of the verifications and prove that it does not belong on your credit report. You can very easily get all three of the credit reports from all three bureaus and dispute the name and social security number as being Totally Incorrect information that is not true and not valid. You must tell them to remove the Totally Incorrect information that does not belong to nor do you have any knowledge of. Tell them also that this information has been misreported and mistakenly put on your credit report! You then dispute every item that is associated with the item. The book teaches this in detail. As far as the student loan business this is covered in the book as well. You can just ignore the collection agencies, there statue of limitations has run out and tell them to do whatever. If I understood correctly, they are threatening to garnish income taxes. Well, this is an old bluff that is always used, although they can do this and it does happen, they can't do it to you. You simply have to tell the collection agencies that you were not even married at the time of the loan and that the loan was never got processed because the school went under. Our book contains a Cease communication letter that I love to send to collection agencies, especially these guys. This letter will legally stop them from ever contacting you again. If they do you can sue them for $1,000.00 right off the bat. it is legal and very effective. You SHOULD NOT have anything that is older than 7 years from the date of last activity on your credit report. If you do simply dispute the information with " this item is totally incorrect and NO Longer valid, remove at once!" This will get the item removed IMMEDIATELY, GUARANTEED!

Watch for incorrect information

Q. will your kit remove credit inquires. I shopped around for a new car and ended up with a lot of inquires that are now hurting my credit.

A. Yes, Inquires can be a real problem for a lot of people. Funny that you mention car dealerships. I specifically talk about car dealerships and inquiries in the book. This is most people acquire about 8 inquiries in one day. The dealerships shop around your credit report, each check with the credit bureaus to see if you qualify for their standards. Most Inquires stay on your credit report for the period of two years. The inquiries that break this rule are inquiries by an existing account such as a visa that is simply checking your current credit status to either make sure you are still a good credit risk or to increase your credit limit. These type of inquiries stay on your credit report for 1 year. You can get rid of the inquiries three different ways. The first by disputing the item under the premise that you have no knowledge of the account and it is misreported. the second by contacting the company that put it on your report and telling them the same thing and that it is effecting your credit report and must be removed immediately. Have that company fax you something stating that it should be removed. The third way is to wait until the two year period is up and dispute it off under the premise that the information is outdated and no longer relevant. Our book shows you step-by-step how to do this and provides you with samples and examples and the forms to do it all. It teaches you this and to much more to mention that the credit bureau wish you didn't know.

"Cut to the Chase"

Cut to the Chase!

This section is great for those who know a little bit about credit and just need the forms and example disputes phrases for specific credit items. I have had an overwhelming response from consumers desiring just the basic information that they would need to know in order to fix a few items on their credit report without having to read an entire book. This approach is for all of the people on the go who really couldn't care less about how the credit system works and all of the ramifications that go along with credit, but simply want to know real quick what they need to do to resolve some undesirable items on their credit. I am going to be very brief and specific. You may have to refer to certain sections in the book to grab a piece of needed information here and there but for the most part that will be up to you if you need it or not. So with that here it is short and sweet.

1) **Get all (3) of your credit reports in front of you.** Refer to the Appendix for exact addresses and phone numbers. The fastest way to get a credit report from Experian and TransUnion is through the Internet. Equifax doesn't allow you to order on-line like the other two but I am sure it won't take them long to get a clue. Here are their web addresses:

   http://www.experian.com/consumer/index.html
   http://www.transunion.com/CreditReport/
   http://www.econsumer.equifax.com/equifax.app/Welcome

2) **Write a Dispute Letter.** Once you get the credit reports you will need to generate/write a dispute letter that is to be sent back to the credit bureau. The key to getting information removed from your credit report is to have it removed via the dispute process; this is the only legal way to change your credit report. I suggest calling the credit bureau in some instances because they can iniate some disputes over the phone once you have the credit report on front of you, be careful on information you give them that you may not want them to know. Either way you must go through all of the credit reports and find all of the items that you believe are incorrect and find a disputable problem with them. You may believe the accuracy of the item to be $0.01 off and this enables you to dispute this item. You need to be a little creative here in wording so that it is considered a legitimate dispute. You will also want to tell them in the dispute to remove the item at once because it is inaccurate and jeopardizing your good credit standing. Refer to Section 4 of the book for example disputes. You will find the samples after each credit item discussed in this section. The example dispute form is located in the Appendix; it also has some sample disputes that you can modify to better fit your particular circumstances. Section 3 of the book details disputing.

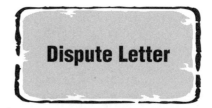

Dispute Letter

The way to cleaning up your credit reports is to obtain them, all (3), and then being clever in disputing certain items that you feel are undesirable. The real key is in the dispute phrase or reason that this item should be removed. All you really want is for the credit bureau to do an investigation on the item with the idea that they may not be able to verify the information as 100% correct, and therefore are deemed by law to remove that item from your credit report because they cannot distribute information they cannot count as true. So get your credit reports, sit down and think about the items that you would just love to have investigated, put it all in a dispute letter and send it right back to the credit bureau. Something important! Whatever you do don't get crazy and try to dispute everything all at once. You need to be realistic and take this in steps. Just like in baseball you don't put every single one of your best hitters all in a row, you need to be strategic and mix things up a little. You put some easy little corrections that I am sure you find obviously wrong with some items on your report with some that you just don't like, but not all at once. Remember, think like an attorney…you have to play by the rules but you the way you say things make all the difference in the world. Good Luck and do take a look at the book when you get a chance it does contain some good information, especially Section 11 "Special Interest."

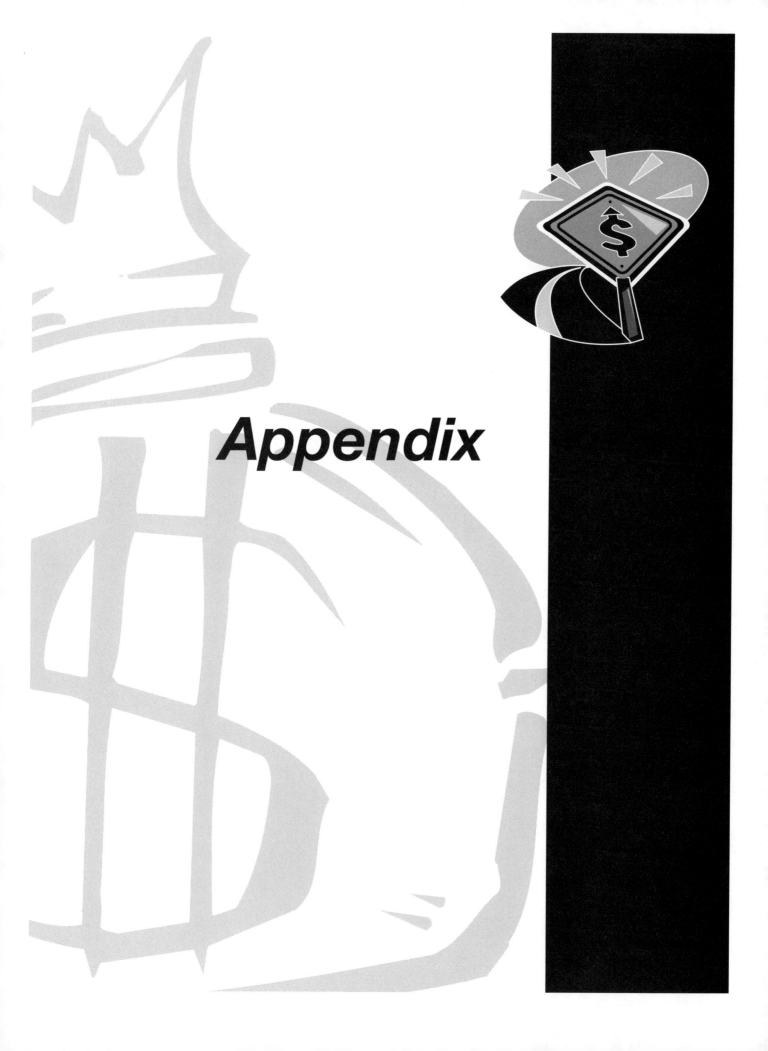

Appendix

Figure No. 1:

THIS FIGURE CONTAINS ALL OF THE PHONE NUMBERS AND ADDRESSES NEEDED TO COR-RESPOND WITH THE CREDIT BUREAUS, CREDITORS, FEDERAL TRADE COMMISSION, AND COLLECTORS. ITEMS IN PARENTHESIS ( ) ARE EITHER INSTRUCTIONS OR HINTS FOR INPUTING INFORMATION IN THAT PARTICULAR AREA.

(To Order Reports)	(To Send Disputes)
EQUIFAX, INC **P.O. BOX 740241** **ATLANTA, GEORGIA 30374**	**EQUIFAX, INC** **P.O. BOX 740256** **ATLANTA, GEORGIA 30374**

To order Equifax Credit Reports by Phone 1-800-997-2493 or http://www.econsumer.equifax.com

(To Order Reports)	(To Send Disputes)
TRANSUNION **P.O. BOX 1000** **CHESTER, PENNSYLVANIA 19022**	**TRANSUNION** **(WEST COAST), P.O. BOX 34012, FULLERTON, CA., 92831** **(EAST COAST), P.O. BOX 2000, CHESTER, PA., 19022**

To order Trans Union Credit Reports by Phone 1-800-888-4213 or http://www.transunion.com

(To Order Reports)	(To Send Disputes)
EXPERIAN **ATTN: NCAC** **P.O. BOX 2002** **ALLEN, TEXAS 75013**	**EXPERIAN** **ATTN: NCAC** **P.O. BOX 2106** **ALLEN, TEXAS 75002**

To order EXPERIAN Credit Reports by Phone 1-888-397-3742 or http://www.experian.com/consumer/index.html

IMPORTANT: MANY STATES HAVE MADE RECENT CHANGES TO THE CREDIT LAWS WHICH ENABLE THE CONSUMER TO RECEIVE A FREE CREDIT REPORT FROM EACH CREDIT BUREAU, EACH YEAR. CHECK WITH EACH CREDIT BUREAU, OR YOUR LOCAL LEGISLATIVE OFFICE TO DETERMINE IF YOUR STATE IS ONE THAT HAS ENACTED THIS LAW. IT WILL MEAN THE DIFFERENCE BETWEEN YOU PAYING FOR A CREDIT REPORT OR RECEIVING IT FREE !!!

Figure No. 1 cont.:

The above addresses and phone numbers represent the largest three credit bureaus. Between the three of these bureaus, they collectively maintain the most accurate information on your credit history. By dealing with these main three bureaus you should be able to rectify your credit history dilemmas. There are many smaller credit bureaus that do exchange your credit history. But these smaller bureaus usually obtain their information from these larger credit bureaus. Thus by correcting the main three you will in turn correct the smaller bureaus. If by chance you encounter a problem with this information, consult the yellow pages under 'CREDIT', for any of the three local credit bureau offices. They can assist you with any further needs.

FOR QUESTIONS OR CONCERNS REGARDING:	PLEASE CONTACT:
CREDIT REPORTING AGENCIES AND CREDITORS	Federal Trade Commision Bureau of Consumer Protection - FCRA Washington, DC 20580 (202) 326-3761
National banks, federal branches/agencies or foreign banks (word "National"or initials "N.A." appear in name)	Office of the Controller of the Currency Compliance Management, Mail Stop 6-6 Washington, DC 20219 1-800-613-6743
Federal Reserve System member banks (except national banks, and federal branches/agencies of foreign banks)	Federal Reserve Board Division of Consumer & Community Affairs Washington, DC 20551 (202) 452-3693
ANY AND ALL TAX QUESTIONS	Internal Revenue Service (IRS) 1-800-829-1040

YOU MAY REFER TO THE WHITE PAGES UNDER FEDERAL GOVERNMENT OFFICES FOR FURTHER INFORMATION AND LOCAL LISTINGS.

Figure No. 2:

TO RECEIVE FREE ANNUAL COPY OF CREDIT REPORT FROM EXPERIAN
(APPLIES ONLY TO A FEW SELECT STATES, i.e. Colorado)

Your Name
Your Address
City, State
Zip Code

Today's Date

EXPERIAN
P.O. Box 949
Allen, TX. 75002

RE: Free annual credit report

To whom it may concern,

I would like to receive my free annual copy of my credit report. The following personal information is provided below, along with my current resident address located above. I have also included a copy of my drivers license or a recent utility bill (reflecting address above).

Here is my personal information:

Full Legal Name: _____

Previous addresses (past 5 years): (It is a good practice to only list one previous address.)

Social Security No.: _____

Date of Birth: _____

Current Employment: (You may choose to list this or not.
                       If you do, you do not have to provide a phone #.)

Thank You,

_____
Your signature   Today's date signed

_____
Your name printed   Today's date printed

Figure No. 3:

TO RECEIVE A PAID COPY OF YOUR CREDIT REPORT FROM EXPERIAN, TRANS UNION, OR EQUIFAX. YOU MUST SEND $8.00 IN WITH YOUR REQUEST. FOR EQUIFAX AND TRANS UNION, YOU ONLY HAVE TO GO BACK (2) YEARS FOR RESIDENCY.

Your Name
Your Address
City, State
Zip Code

Today's Date

USE THE ADDRESSES IN FIGURE 1
FOR EACH CREDIT BUREAU
YOU ARE WRITING TO.

RE: Request for credit report

To whom it may concern,

I would like to receive a copy of my credit report. The following personal information is provided below, along with my current resident address located above. I have also included $8.00, a copy of my drivers license or recent utility bill (reflecting address above).

Here is my personal information:

Full Legal Name: _____

Previous addresses (past 2 or 5 years): (It is a good practice to only list one previous address.)

Social Security No.: _____

Date of Birth: _____

Current Employment: (You may choose to list this or not. _____
                     If you do, you do not have to provide a phone #.)

Thank You,

_____
Your signature   Today's date signed

_____
Your name printed   Today's date printed

Figure No. 4:

TO REQUEST A FREE CREDIT REPORT IF YOU HAVE BEEN DENIED INSURANCE, EMPLOY-MENT, OR CREDIT WITHIN THE PAST 60 DAYS. FOR EQUIFAX AND TRANS UNION YOU ONLY HAVE TO GO BACK (2) YEARS FOR RESIDENCY.

Your Name
Your Address
City, State
Zip Code

Today's Date

USE THE ADDRESSES IN FIGURE 1
FOR EACH CREDIT BUREAU
YOU ARE WRITING TO.

RE: Request for A FREE credit report

To whom it may concern,

I was recently denied (credit, insurance, employment) by (whomever denied you) due to information obtained through (credit bureau name). In lieu of this recent denial, I would appreciate a free copy of my credit report. I have provided all of my most recent personal information below, along with my current resident address located above. I have also included a copy of my drivers license or current utility bill (reflecting address above), along with the denial letter from (whoever denied you).

Here is my personal information:

Full Legal Name: _____

Previous addresses (past 2 or 5 years): (It is a good practice to only list one previous address.)

Social Security No.:_____

Date of Birth: _____

Current Employment: (You may choose to list this or not. _____
                     If you do, you do not have to provide a phone #.)

Thank You,

_____
Your signature   Today's date signed

_____
Your name printed   Today's date printed

Figure No. 5:

DISPUTE LETTER (note: certain business names have been misspelled on purpose)

Your Name
Your Address
City, State
Zip Code

Today's Date

USE THE ADDRESSES IN FIGURE 1
FOR EACH CREDIT BUREAU
YOU ARE WRITING TO.

RE: DISPUTE AND/OR CORRECT ERRONEOUS ITEMS ON CREDIT REPORT

To whom it may concern,

I have gone through my credit report and distinguished every line of information that I believe to be erroneous, outdated, or simply mishandled and incorrectly recorded. Each item on the original credit report has been numbered. The items being disputed have been Hi-lited on the original credit report for reference purposes. I will work sequentially through the items Hi-lited on the credit report, beginning with the lowest item number being disputed. Each item referenced will correspond to the number designated on my credit report. I will then address the problem that exists with each item. Verification of recorded documentation will reveal the legitimacy to the disputed items. It is of my deepest concern that this matter can be corrected without much difficulty, and I can begin restoring my credit integrity.

Here is my personal information:

Full Legal Name: _____

Previous addresses (past 2 or 5 years): (It is a good practice to only list one previous address.)

Social Security No.: _____

Date of Birth: _____

Current Employment: (You may choose to list this or not.
                     If you do, you do not have to provide a phone #.)

ITEM: (These are the items you have numbered and hi-lited on your credit report.)

1) Fill in these areas with a variation of the sample phrases that apply to each of your credit dilemmas.

2) Be creative in your own dispute phrases, so that it doesn't look exactly like mine.

App-9

Figure No. 5 cont.:

3) Remember, if they think you are pulling their leg, they will not change a single thing. Thank you very much for your time and patience. I hope these problems can be rectified as soon as possible. I appreciate your cooperation.

Sincerely,

_____

Your signature   Today's date signed

_____

Your name printed   Today's date printed

HERE ARE SOME EXAMPLE DISPUTE PHRASES FOR COMMON PROBLEMS
(The following examples purposely contain fictitious names of creditors)

2) Acct # XXXXXXXXXXXX with American Expresso is erroneous in that it indicates full payment was received 120+ days late (05 status), and was subsequently turned over to a collection agency. This account was paid off in full in a timely manner and closed at my request. A **'01 status'** should replace the **'05 status'**. Please update this information to reflect such actions or **remove this item entirely.**

5) Acct # XXXXXXXXXXXX with Saers is erroneous. This account does not belong to me. Verification of signed documentation will reveal such validity. Please **remove this account and it's inaccuracies at once.**

7) Acct # XXXXXXXX with JKPenney Inc. is erroneous in it's MOP status of '03'. This information is incorrect as verification to the legitimacy to this dispute will indicate. Please **remove the MOP note '03' from this item and replace it with '01'.**

8) Acct # XXXXX with Pacefec Credit Bureau (PCB) is erroneous and should be removed. I contacted PCB and found that this delinquent account is for a Pacific Bell phone bill, located in California. Even though my social security No. is accurate, there must be a mix-up between my father and me who has the exactly the same name, and who resides in Northridge California. I have no knowledge of this account and believe it to be fraudulent. Firstly, I have resided in **Colorado** for all of my life. Secondly, at the exact time as indicated on this report, I resided at 1111 W. Somewhere Dr., Denver Co. 80204, and had phone service with U.S. West Comm.. This information can be verified by simply examining every other item on my credit report, and noting the dates and address established by these accounts. This item is not at all accurate, **please remove it from my credit report at once.**

10 & 11) Acct # XXXXXXXXXX-X with Nationnel Account Adjusters (NAA) is not correct and/or valid. NAA was contacted and it was discovered that the information in their position is not accurate and very incomplete, to say the least. As far as what NAA can understand, an error was made on the part of The University of Colorado Denver-Office of Financial Aid. The error originates from Bursars office of UCD mishandling properly filed financial aid records, giving them the **false** impression that was an outstanding tuition balance that was never paid. Once their financial aid records were rectified to reflect that the tuition and all fees were covered by Government Aid and I was free of responsibility, my account had already been referred to NAA. Although NAA was contacted by UCD and notified that all payments were received and that this account should be closed and noted as in good standing, it had already been reported to Credit Bureau. This account on my credit report is incorrect and unsubstantiated. **Please verify and remove these items at once.**

Figure No. 5 cont.:

13) This **Judgment** is not correct and does not apply to me. Continenntel Collections was recently contacted and it was discovered that the information contained in their records was not correct and I was released of all responsibility. **Please remove this item at once.**

16) Acct # XXXXX with Callection Assoc. Inc. is erroneous and **does not belong to me**. This item indicates an outstanding bill to Have Mercy Hospital. I have no knowledge of this matter and believe it to be inaccurate. Please **remove this item from my credit report.**

18) Acct # XXXX with Orange Tiger Collections is erroneous and **does not belong to me**. I spoke with a Who Ever of the above mentioned who stated that there exists a discrepancy with names. I have no knowledge of this account, please **remove this account at once.**

20) Acct # XXXXXXXXX Mele Hi Cablevision is erroneous and **does not belong to me**. I contacted the above mentioned and was able to learn that the account was registered to a Mr. Somebody living at 35111 Vallejo St., Denver Co.. I don't know this person and never lived at this address. I have never had an account with Mele Hi Cablevision. Please **remove this item at once.**

21) I never applied to Signet Bank/ Virginia, nor have I ever lived in Virginia. Please **remove this inquiry at once.**

4) This Bankruptcy listed on my credit report is inaccurate nor valid. I never filed a bankruptcy on this date or in this amount. Please **remove this item at once!**

6) The Lien listed on my credit report filed on 1/5/96 in Fulton Cty is not at all accurate and completely erroneous. Please **remove this item at once!**

8) I never had or filed a Foreclosure. This information is inaccurate and unsubstantiated. Please **remove this totally erroneous item at once!**

10) Acct # XXX-XXXX with ABC Collections is erroneous in it's validity. ABC Collections was contacted and it was discovered that this item indicates an ambulance bill that was never paid. This information is not at all accurate. I never consented to any type of ambulance service. Verification of documentation will indicate that this item is unsubstantiated and erroneous. **Please remove this item at once!**

12) The Repossession listed is not all accurate and **does not belong to me**. I never owned a Ford Explorer, let alone had it repossessed. This information is erroneous, **Please remove this item at once!**

It is legally within your rights of the law to have any item you feel, for what ever reason you may feel it, to be disputed and verified by the Credit Bureau handling your records. Even if you know that the account or item belongs to you, but you just have a very slight feeling about it's true accuracy, you can present the credit bureau with a legitimate request asking them to verify an item. This request forces the credit bureau to, in other words "prove it". If 100% documented accuracy isn't discovered within 30 days discrediting your dispute, or proving it to you, this account legitimate or not MUST be removed by law. So if for WHAT EVER reason it doesn't get verified within 30 days, a computer system down, the business no longer exists or has moved and can't be located, lost file, nobody means to do verifications, court house personnel to busy with more important things to do, account has a previous name associated with it, wrong account #'s, it MUST BE REMOVED!!!

Figure No. 6:

CEASECOMM LETTER THIS ITEM MUST BE SENT BY CERTIFIED MAIL!!!

VIA CERTIFIED MAIL RRR # (PUT THE NUMBER OF THE CERTIFIED MAIL RECEIPT HERE)

YOUR NAME
YOUR ADDRESS
CITY, STATE, ZIP CODE

Today's Date

SAMPLE Credit Services (place collector here)
P.O. Box 1212
Lostin, Il. 60006-1538

RE: Acct.# S5222-01-2222 / Student Loan / $2449.65

Dear Debt Collection Agency:

This will serve as your legal notice under federal law, The Fair Debt Collection Act, to cease all communication with me in reference to the above account.

If you fail to head this notice, I will file a formal complaint against you with the Federal Trade Commission who is responsible for enforcement, and the American Collectors Association, and the State Attorney General's Office.

I have decided that we do not desire to work with a collection agency under any circumstance. We will contact the U.S. Dept. Of Education to resolve this matter directly.

You are also notified that if any adverse items are placed against my credit report as a result of this notice, I will be forced to take appropriate action against you, and concerned parties.

Give this matter the attention it deserves.

Yours Truly,

_____
Your signature   Today's date signed

_____
Your name   Today's date printed

Figure No. 7 :

COMPROMISE LETTER THIS ITEM MUST BE SENT BY CERTIFIED MAIL!!!

VIA CERTIFIED MAIL RRR # (PUT THE NUMBER OF THE CERTIFIED MAIL RECEIPT HERE)

YOUR NAME
YOUR ADDRESS
CITY, STATE, ZIP CODE

Today's Date

SAMPLE Credit (place creditor here)
P.O. Box 1212
Lostin, Il. 60006-1538

RE: Acct.# 5555554441

Dear who ever you spoke with:

As we discussed, I became unemployed and was no longer able to pay on my account. As a result, the above mentioned account was sent to collection (or charged off) by your company.

Since then, I have obtained a very rewarding and stable job. I would now like to either resume payments on this account at $(however much) per month, or simply pay the account in full.

I recently obtained a copy of my credit report and noted that your company has reported this account as: (delinquent, sent to collections). I wish to bring this account or matter to a resolution that will be fair, and beneficial for both of us. I hereby propose to pay you: X monthly payments of $money, or remit a check to you in the amount of $debt as payment in full provided you are willing to send me a letter stating you will report this to any and all credit reporting agencies as: 'PAID AS AGREED' or notify me in writing that you agree to delete this item from any and all credit reporting agencies.

Due to the inequities of the system I AM NOT agreeable to accepting a 'PAID P & L' or 'CHARGE OFF' for an additional amount of time on my credit report. It is my position that I have suffered enough as a result of this problem.

Upon receipt of your letter I will forward you a cashier's check or money order in the amount of $debt.
Yours Truly,

Your signature   Today's date signed

Your name   Today's date printed

Banks Offering Unsecured Credit Cards

Institution	A.P.R.	Annual Fee	Credit Line	Phone Number
Aria Visa Personal (Providean)	23.99%	$89	$250 - $25,000	888-237-4837
Advanta National Bank	11.9%	$20	$250-$3000	800-833-6980
1st Financial Bank USA Dakota	16.06%	$0	$250-$4000	530-672-7700
Associated Card Service Bank	16.65%	$15	$200-$3500	800-472-7708
Associates National Bank (DE)	19.7%	$30	$250-$5000	800-533-5600
Capital One bank	9.9%	$0	$250-$25,000	800-955-7070
Chase Manhattan Bank	15.4%	$0	$200 - $25,000	800-441-7681
Corestates Bank of Delaware	17.03%	$20	$250-$2500	800-833-3010
Cross Country Bank	20.99%	$50	$250-$3500	302-326-4200
First Premier Bank	19.9%	$60*	$250 - $2500	605-335-2255
First Consumers National Bank	17.24%	$0	$250 - $2500	800-211-7339
First National Bank of Marin	19.80%	$72	$250-$3500	800-752-5493
First USA bank	9.99%	$0	$250-$25,000	800-347-7887
MBNA America Bank	14.99%	$0	$250-$25,000	800-847-7378
Nationsbank of Delaware	14.4%	$0	$250-$10,000	800-582-6230
Providean Bank	14.99%	$25	$250-$3500	800-664-2614
Sterling Bank & Trust	19.9%	$39	$250 - $5000	800-767-0923

Banks Offering Secured Credit Cards

Institution	A.P.R.	Annual Fee	Deposit / INT	Phone Number
American Pacific Bank	17.40%	$25	$400 / MR	800-610-1201
Associates National Bank	19.80%	$25	$300 / 4.53%	800-884-1832
AT&T Universal Card Services	20.40%	$20	$300 / 3.35%	800-423-4343
Bank of Hoven Card Services	19.80%	$39	$380 / 4.6%	800-777-7735
Bank One Arizona	19.90%	$25	$250 / 4.0%	800-544-4110
Capital One	19.80%	$29	$99 / Varies	888-505-9573
Chase (USA)	17.90%	$20	$300 / 4.0%	800-482-4273
Chevy Chase Bank	22.60%	$35	$300 / 4.0%	800-556-6333
Citibank	17.90%	$20	$300 / 4.0%	800-743-1332
Citizens Financial Group	15.65%	$25	$300 / 1.50%	800-922-9999
Community Bank	15.90%	$29	$300 / 1.50%	800-779-8472
Cross Country Bank	19.00%	$39	$200 / 3.0%	800-262-3610
Federal Savings Bank	9.72%	$39*	$250 / 2.5%	800-290-9060
First Consumers National Bank	19.00%	$39	$100 / 2.22%	800-876-3262
First Omni Bank	15.49%	None	$300 / Varies	800-441-8026
First National Bank in Brookings	18.90%	$35*	$250 / 4.0%	800-658-3660
First Premier Bank	21.00%	$69*	$200 / None	800-987-5521
Key Bank and Trust	18.50%	$45	$300 / 2.25%	800-333-VISA
Marine Midland	19.90%	$40	$200 / Varies	800-539-5398
Orchard Bank	19.80%	$35	$300 / Varies	800-962-7463
Peoples Bank	18.90%	$35	$200 / 2.0%	800-488-2720
Sterling Bank & Trust	16.90%	$25	$500 / 2.0%	800-262-4442
United National Bank	18.90%	$35	$500 / Varies	800-628-8946

The above mentioned banks offer secured and unsecured credit cards for individuals with past credit problems or no credit at all. There are a few banks across the country that do not require a security deposit in order to obtain approval, but some unfortunately do. However acquiring a secured credit card is a great way to start building your credit rating. If you are at least 18 years of age, have a residency with a telephone, and earn at least $1000 per month (household income), you may be approved for one of these unsecured credit cards. The income qualifications that each of the above banks require for approval may differ, so please call them to see if you qualify. Interest rates, annual fees and credit lines for the above listed banks may change.

* The asterisks next to the fees above simply mean that some of these banks may have additional fees that apply, so be sure to ask them about additional fees.

Glossary of Credit Terms

A

Annual Fees - A yearly fee charged by credit grantors for the privilege of using a credit card.
Annual Percentage Rate - The cost of credit at a yearly rate.
Applicant - A person applying for credit privileges, employment or some other benefit.
Asset - Any thing you own that has value or use.
Authorized Account User - The person authorized by the contractually responsible party to use the account.

B

Bankruptcy - A proceeding in U.S. Federal Court that may legally release a person from repaying debts owed. The law contains several chapters which relate to different methods of relief:

Chapter 7 - Straight Bankruptcy (total liquidation of assets)
Chapter 11 - Business Reorganizations
Chapter 12 - Farm Debt Bankruptcy
Chapter 13 - Wage Earner Repayment Plan

Bankruptcy Discharged - A court order terminating bankruptcy proceedings on old debts.
Bankruptcy Dismissed - A court order that denied a bankruptcy petition making the debtor still liable for all debts.
Budget A - financial plan for saving and spending money.

C

Charge Card - A card which requires payment in full upon receipt of the statement.
Charge Off -Accounting term to indicate that the creditor does not expect to collect the balance owed on an account.
Collection Account -An account which has been transferred from a routine debt to a Collection Department of the creditors firm or to a separate professional debt collecting firm.
Consolidation Loan - A loan usually obtained for the purpose of reducing the amount of the payments of bills owed by consolidating the bills into one loan payment. The consumer pays off several bills with the proceeds from one loan and is left with one consolidated monthly payment.
Collateral - Property acceptable as security for a loan or other obligation.
Consumer - Person who uses and/or buys goods and services for family or personal use.
Consumer Credit Counseling Service - Organizations which help consumers find a way to repay debts through careful budgeting and management of funds. These are usually nonprofit organizations, funded by creditors. By requesting that creditors accept a longer pay-off period, the counseling services can often design a successful repayment plan.
Co-Signer - Person responsible for repaying a debt if the borrower defaults.
Credit -A trust or a promise to pay later for goods or services purchased today.
Credit Card -A rectangular piece of plastic used instead of cash or checks authorizing payment for goods and services.
Credit Grantor - Person or business furnishing consumer goods and/or services on credit.
Credit HistoryRecord of how a consumer has paid credit accounts in the past, used as a guide to determine whether the consumer is likely to pay accounts on time in the future.
Credit LimitThe maximum amount of money which can be charged on a particular credit account.

Credit Report - A record or file to a prospective lender or employer on the credit standing of a prospective borrower, used to help determine credit worthiness.

Credit Reporting Agency - A company which gathers, files and sells information to creditors and/or employers to facilitate their decisions to extend credit or to hire.

D

Debit Card Purchases - are deducted directly from the consumer's personal checking account.

B

Equal Credit Opportunity Act (ECOA) - A federal law that requires lenders and other creditors to make credit equally available without discrimination based on race, color, religion, national origin, age, sex, marital status, or receipt of income from public assistance programs.

Equifax- One of the three major credit reporting agencies, headquartered in Atlanta, Georgia.

Experian - One of the three major credit reporting agencies, formerly known as TRW.

F

Fair Credit Reporting Act - A federal law, established in 1971, and revised in 1997, which enables consumers to learn what information Credit Reporting Agencies have on file about them, and to dispute inaccurate data in the file. It also establishes specific permissible purposes for which credit reports may be requested, and places time limits on how long adverse information may be reported.

G

Garnishment - Legal process whereby a creditor has obtained judgment on a debt may obtain full or partial payment by seizure of a portion of a debtor's assets (wages, bank account, etc.).

Grace Period - The period allowed to avoid any finance charges by paying off the balance in full before the due date.

Home Equity Loan - A loan based on the difference of the amount of equity paid on a home, and the home's current market value.I

Installment Loan - A credit account in which the amount of the payment and the number of payments are predetermined or fixed.

Interest - The cost of borrowing or lending money, usually a percentage of the amount borrowed or loaned.

J

Judgment - The official court decision of an action or suit. This public record may be listed on a credit report in matters of money and debts owed.

L

Lease -A written document containing the conditions under which the possession and use of real and/or personal property are given by the owner to another for a stated period and for a stated consideration.

Lien - A legal hold or claim of one person on the property of another as security for a debt or charge. The right given by law to satisfy debt. (A lien must be paid and released).

M

Mortgage - A lien or claim against real property given by the buyer to the lender as security for money borrowed.

1st Mortgage-Also known as the "primary" mortgage-has priority over the claims of subsequent lenders for the same property.

2nd Mortgage-Also know as the "secondary" mortgage-is a loan secured by mortgage or trust deed, which lien is "junior" to another mortgage or trust.

P

Permissible Purposes - As defined in section 604 of the Fair Credit Reporting Act, only the named reasons for requesting a credit report are deemed "permissible". Requests not meeting these criteria must be denied.

Personal Line of Credit - The maximum amount one can owe at any time, based on income, debt and credit history.

Personal Loan - A loan based on a consumer's income, debt and credit history.

Principal -The outstanding balance of a loan, exclusive of interest and other charges.

Public Record - Information obtained by the Credit Reporting Agency from court records, such as liens, bankruptcy filings and judgments. Public records are open to any person who requests them.

R

Repossession - Forced, or voluntary surrender of merchandise as a result of the customer's failure to pay as promised. There are several types and descriptions of repossession actions.

Revolving Account - An account which requires at least a specified minimum payment each month plus a service charge on the balance. As the balance declines, the amount of the service charge, or interest, also declines.

S

Secured Credit Card - A credit card secured by a savings account that has been established in advance by the borrower. The amount in the account usually determines the limit on the credit card. These accounts present no real risk factor for creditors and are therefore much easier to obtain.

Smart Card - An electronic prepaid cash card, usually sold at banks and exchanged at face value.

T

Trans Union -One of the three major Credit Reporting Agencies.